M000085625

ISLAM AND THE WEST:
CONFLICT, COEXISTENCE
OR CONVERSION?

"A timely book . . . Chapman's thesis is that people living in a multi-ethnic society are not doomed to confront or to ignore one another . . . Will Christians, Muslims, people of other faiths and of no faith at all rise to the challenge and engage in a genuine dialogue?"
Dr Chawkat Moucarry, Lecturer in Islamics at All Nations Christian College.

ISLAM AND THE WEST:
CONFLICT, COEXISTENCE
OR CONVERSION?

Colin Chapman

paternoster press

Copyright © 1998 Colin Chapman

First published in 1998 by Paternoster Press

04 03 02 01 00 99 98   7 6 5 4 3 2 1

Paternoster Press is an imprint of Paternoster Publishing,
PO Box 300, Carlisle, Cumbria, CA3 0QS, UK
http://www.paternoster-publishing.com

The right of Colin Chapman to be identified as the Author of this work
has been asserted by him in accordance with Copyright, Designs and
Patents Act 1988.

*All rights reserved. No part of this publication may be reproduced,
stored in a retrieval system, or transmitted in any form or by any
means, electronic, mechanical, photocopying, recording or otherwise,
without the prior permission of the publisher or a licence permitting
restricted copying. In the UK such licences are issued by the
Copyright Licensing Agency,
90 Tottenham Court Road, London W1P 9HE.*

British Library Cataloguing in Publication Data

A catalogue record for this book is available from the British Library.

ISBN 0-85364-781-X

Cover design by Mainstream, Lancaster
Typeset by WestKey Ltd, Falmouth, Cornwall
Printed in Great Britain by Clays Ltd, St Ives plc

Contents

Acknowledgements

Akbar Ahmed, *Discovering Islam: Making Sense of Muslim History and Society*, pp. 65–66, 67, published in 1988 and reproduced with the permission of the publisher, Routledge, London.

Zaki Badawi, *Islam in Britain*, pp. 26–7, published in 1981 and reproduced with the permission of the publishers, Ta Ha Publishers, London.

K. Bailey, *Poet and Peasant, and Through Peasant Eyes*, p. 206, published in 1983 and reproduced with the permission of the publisher, W.M.B. Eerdmans, Grand Rapids, MI.

K. Cragg, *The Call of the Minaret*, pp. 6–8, published in 1986 and reproduced with the permission of the publisher, Harper Collins, London.

Ali Köse, *Conversion to Islam: A Study of Native British Converts*, published in 1996. Extracts reproduced with the permission of the publisher, Kegan Paul International, London.

E.A. Meyer, *Islam and Human Rights: Tradition and Politics*, published in 1995 by Pinter, London, an imprint of Cassell. Extracts reproduced by permission of the publisher Cassell, Wellington House, 125 Strand, London, WC2R 0BB, England.

O. Roy, *The Failure of Political Islam* published in 1994. Extracts reproduced with the permission of the publishers, I.B. Tauris & Co Ltd, London.

W. Montgomery Watt, 'Islam and the West', in *Islam in the Modern World*, p. 3, D. MacEoin and Ahmed Al-Shahi (eds.) published in 1983. Extract reproduced with the permission of the publisher, Croom Helm, London and Canberra.

W. Montgomery Watt, *Islamic Political Thought: The Basic Concepts*, pp. 18–19, published in 1968 and reproduced with the permission of the publishers, Edinburgh University Press, Edinburgh.

Seyyed Hossein Nasr, 'Islam and the West: yesterday and today', Q-News International No. 248–50 (Dec 96–Jan 97), extracts reprinted with the permission of the publisher, The American Journal of Islamic Social Sciences, Herdon, VA.

Series Preface

Easneye is the name of a small hill on the edge of the river Lea, twenty-five miles north of London between the town of Ware and the village of Stanstead Abbotts in Hertfordshire, England. It was purchased in 1867 by the son of Sir Thomas Fowell Buxton, 'The Liberator', who had been responsible, with William Wilberforce, for the abolition of the slave trade. The beautiful house portrayed on the back cover was completed in 1869 and remained the home of the Buxton family and the hub of their broad missionary and philanthropic involvements for several generations.

Since 1971 Easneye has been the home of **All Nations Christian College** which, since its foundation in 1923, has been training people for cross-cultural Christian mission – people who continue to come from all over the world and to go to the ends of the earth for the sake of the gospel.

The Easneye Lectures are delivered as an annual series at All Nations by a visiting guest lecturer who is noted in the field of missiology. The purpose of the Lectures is to enhance the level of theological reflection on the practice of mission, to explore the riches of mission history throughout the world, and to contribute to current debates surrounding missiological issues and challenges.

Lady Hannah Buxton, widow of Sir Thomas, in a letter written to her grandson on 8 May 1869, expressed this prayer for the fine building at Easneye:

That it may ever be inhabited by faithful servants of God in and through Christ Jesus, and that it may ever be a habitation of God in the hearts of the inhabitants by the Holy Spirit, and Christ be honoured, confessed and served, and this place be a fountain of blessing in the church and in the world.

This vision constantly inspires those who live, work and study at All Nations, and the **Easneye Lectures** are prepared and published in the same spirit.

Chris Wright

Introduction

The Muslim East and the Christian West . . . have been living in confrontation and conflict for centuries (Khurram Murad).[1]

The two communities have been yoked together through cooperation and conflict, tolerance and hatred, dialogue and diatribe, personal friendship and communal strife (Philip Hitti).[2]

On the threshold of the 21st century the confrontation between Islam and the West poses terrible internal dilemmas for both . . . It is an apocalyptic test; the most severe examination (Akbar S. Ahmed).[3]

A long and intimate, an ambiguous and usually painful relationship (Albert Hourani).[4]

Whether we look backwards or forwards in time, it is hard to get away from the words 'conflict' and 'confrontation' when thinking about the relationship between Islam and the West. But while they sum up important aspects of the encounter over the past fourteen hundred years, they certainly don't tell the whole story. There have been times of genuine coexistence, and if the rhetoric about 'the clash of civilizations' is challenged, we can perhaps look forward to a more positive relationship in the future. But where in this scenario might 'conversion' fit in? Is it a question of Islam converting the West? Or is there any possibility that the conversion might work the other way round, and that Islam might somehow be changed through its contact with the West?

We cannot even begin our enquiry, however, until we recognize the difficulty in using the term 'Islam'. 'Is it', asks Seyyed Hossein Nasr,

> traditional Islam as practised by the majority of Muslims, the Islam of the pious men and women who seek to live in the light of God's teaching as revealed in the Qur'an and in surrender to His will? Or is it the modernist interpretations that seem to interpret the Islamic tradition in view of currently prevalent Western ideas and fashions of thought? Or yet, is it the extreme forms of politically active Islam . . .[5]

The same kind of questions would need to be asked about 'the West': is it the Judaeo-Christian tradition that has been at the heart of European Christendom and is now represented by a small remnant of Jews and Christians, and exercising a certain influence in public life? Or is it the secular humanism that developed out of the Renaissance and the Enlightenment and looks as if it has conquered much of the world? Can the West still in any sense be described as 'Christian' (as most Muslims seem to assume), or should it simply be labelled 'post-Christian' (as most people in the West tend to think)? Nasr's perception as a Muslim is that 'Christianity presents itself to Islam as a powerful spiritual force that, in reality, still dominates the West'. At the same time he is very aware that 'much of Christian theology is changing with incredible rapidity, and what has survived of Christian ethics in Western society is disappearing apace'.[6] When we speak of 'the West', therefore, should we be thinking not so much about religion and ideology but rather about the political power, the science and technology, the media and the pop culture which are exported all over the world?

The coming of Islam to the West in recent years has introduced a significantly new dynamic into this situation. William Montgomery Watt, the well-known Christian Islamicist who taught in Edinburgh for decades, was in no doubt about the seriousness of the challenge to Christianity when he wrote in 1976: 'It is hardly too much to say that the intellectual challenge to Christianity from Islam at the present time is greater than any challenge Christians have had to meet for fifteen centuries, not excluding that from the natural sciences.'[7]

The challenge presented to the secular West is just as far-reaching, as Lamin Sanneh explains:

> The Muslim challenge in asserting a religious interest in government and education may be considered a challenge also to the prevailing Western attitude of secular accommodation, or even abdication. Consequently, behind the back of a Christian religious retreat from the public square comes a rising tide of Muslim demands for a role for religion in public affairs. Islam has always conceived a political role for religion, whatever the ambivalence of individual Muslims. However, what is new and different now is that the Muslim pressure is being brought to bear in the West itself, and is not simply a matter confined to distant and exotic societies ... Westerners are caught in a bind in the face of Muslim demands; the logic of religious toleration, not to say of hospitality, requires making concessions to Muslims, while the logic of privatizing Christianity, of taking religion out of the public arena, disqualifies Westerners from dealing in any effective sense with Muslim theocratic demands.[8]

The eight chapters of this book are an expansion of a series of four lectures given at All Nations Christian College as the Easneye lectures from 26 to 29 February 1996. In the first of the lectures I began by recognizing the enormity and complexity of the subject, and expressed the hope that the college might join with others to set up a multidisciplinary study project to pursue different aspects of this same theme. Since the consultation on 'Faith and Power: Christianity and Islam in Britain', which was held at the Institute for Contemporary Christianity in London on 3 and 4 November 1997, took up many of these themes, there seems a real possibility that such a process can be launched in the not-too-distant future.

Each chapter in the book concentrates on one particular aspect of the meeting between Islam and the West at the present time. Taken together, I hope they may suggest a kind of framework within which this kind of exploration can be continued – ideally with Christians and Muslims working together.

Chapter 1 (**The Legacy of History: No End to an Uneasy Relationship?**) looks at the history of the last fourteen hundred years, exploring memories inherited on both sides from the past, and noting some of the complex factors which affect the attitudes and feelings of all the parties involved in the meeting of Islam and the West.

Chapter 2 (**Islamic Mission in the Past: Persuasion without Compulsion?**) reflects on the way Islam spread in the Middle East and other parts of the world, attempting to understand why so many left other religions in favour of Islam; this inevitably raises the question of whether a similar process is likely to be repeated in the West today.

Chapter 3 (**Islamic Mission Today: is the West Ripe for Conversion?**) reflects on the experience of individual converts in recent years, seeking to understand what has led them to turn from a previous faith or no faith to accept the religion of Islam.

Chapter 4 (**The War of Words: Polemics, Apologetics or Dialogue?**) is a study of the variety of ways in which Christians in the past and present have tried to engage in debate and dialogue with the faith of Islam at a theological level.

Chapter 5 (**Human Rights: A Conflict between Secular and Islamic Concepts?**) explores ways in which the secular West and Islam approach questions of human rights today, asking whether there is genuine common ground between the two approaches, or whether they are starting from fundamentally different assumptions.

Chapter 6 (**Education: From Demand to Dialogue?**) focuses on the world of education, especially in British schools, attempting to understand and respond to Muslim demands in this area.

Chapter 7 (**Establishment: Does the Islamic Presence Alter the Equation?**) opens up the debate about the relationship between church and state in Britain, asking whether the presence of Islam in Britain should make any difference to strongly held opinions for and against establishment.

Chapter 8 (**Hopes for the Future: Dialogue on a More Level Playing Field?**) makes a plea for a more intensive dialogue at many levels between Muslims, Christians and secularists in the West.

Notes

1   Khurram Murad in *Muslims in the West: the message and the mission*, Syed Abul Hasan Ali Nadwi, edited by Khurram Murad, The Muslim Foundation, Leicester, 1983, p. 25.
2   Philip Hitti, *Islam and the West*, Van Nostrand, Princeton, 1962, p. 6.
3   Akbar S. Ahmed, 'Muslim Education and the Impact of the Western Mass Media', *Muslim Educational Quarterly*, vol. 11, no. 3, 1994, The Islamic Academy, Cambridge, UK, p. 31.
4   Albert Hourani, *Europe and the Middle East*, Macmillan, London, 1980, pp. 71–2.
5   Seyyed Hossein Nasr, 'Islam and the West: yesterday and today', *Q-News International*, No. 248–50, 27 Dec 1996–9 Jan 1997, p. 10.
6   Ibid., p. 41.
7   William Montgomery Watt, *Times Literary Supplement*, 30 April 1976, p. 513.
8   Lamin Sanneh, 'Can a House Divided Stand? Reflections on Christian-Muslim encounter in the West', *International Bulletin of Missionary Research*, Oct 1993, p. 164.

One

The Legacy of History: No End to an Uneasy Relationship?

Introduction

> The communities which profess the two religions have faced each other across the Mediterranean, for more than a thousand years; with hostility, it is true, but with a look of recognition in their eyes (Albert Hourani).[1]

> The starting point for improving relationships between the Muslim and Western worlds should be an objective appraisal of present-day realities, including those areas of agreement and divergence between them. While no one can totally ignore history, it would be a tragedy if we became prisoners of the past (Khurshid Ahmad).[2]

> It is crucial that the potential points of conflict are identified if continued confrontation is to be avoided (Akbar S. Ahmed).[3]

Any attempt to study the meeting of Islam and the West today must begin with history. In no country of the world can Christians and Muslims forget their past and act as if nothing has happened between them. Memories of the past colour every relationship between individuals and communities on both sides in one way or another, so that wherever we turn we become aware of what Seyyed Hossein Nasr calls 'a depository of historical memories to which interested parties and groups can always appeal to fan the fire of hatred and to create a false image of a powerful enemy'.[4]

It is vital that our historical memory should embrace the positive as well as the negative. For, as Khurshid Ahmad reminds us,

> military encounters have not been the whole story; there have also been long spells of diplomatic understandings, trade relations, intellectual cross-fertilizations, the sharing of scientific and technological developments, and cultural exchanges. Understandably, there have been periods of rivalry and confrontation; but there have also been eras of peace and tranquility. Islam and the West have not been merely 'civilizations at war'; they have also been 'partners in history'.[5]

Our task, however, is not to chronicle particular events, but rather to recognize the impressions that have been left on the memory of the main parties concerned. It is particularly important that people in the West should be able to listen with greater sympathy to Muslim interpretations of history. Two recent articles by Muslim writers on this theme are particularly valuable for this purpose, and will be quoted at some length. The first is an article by Khurshid Ahmad of Pakistan on 'Islam and the West: confrontation or cooperation?' which appeared in the *Muslim World* in 1995. The second is by the Iranian Seyyed Hossein Nasr, entitled 'Islam and the West: yesterday and today', which was originally published in the *American Journal of Islamic Social Sciences* in 1996, and reprinted in the British Muslim journal, *Q News International*, in December 1996. While in some cases they express purely personal views, they generally reflect accurately the views of a wide spectrum of Muslims. Although it is tempting to respond to many of their observations and interpretations, we refrain from doing so because it is important that people in the West should feel the full force of Muslim views on these subjects.[6]

After a brief survey of six major periods of engagement, we attempt to list some of the main factors relating to both politics and theology that affect the ways in which 'the West' and 'Islam' view each other today. We shall see that while many of these reveal the potential for confrontation, others point to areas in which there is real hope of mutual understanding between 'Islam' and, if not all, at least some, in 'the West'.

1. Memories inherited from the past

(i) Early conquest and the Islamic Empire

One of the first recorded contacts at an official level between Islam and a European power came in the letter sent by the Prophet Muhammad through his ambassadors to Heraclius, ruler of the eastern Roman Empire, in Byzantium on 11 May AD 628, four years before the Prophet's death. In this letter he invited him to accept Islam with the words 'I call you to Allah ... And I invite you and your people to Allah, Mighty, Sublime. I have done my duty of conveying the Message and the counsel, so accept my advice . . .' Khurshid Ahmad describes the Emperor's response as 'gentle'.[7]

Soon after the death of Muhammad in 632, the Arab armies extended their rule all over the middle East and north Africa, establishing an Empire in which the majority of their subjects were (at least initially) Jewish, Christian or Zoroastrian. The Christian communities that have survived to the present day in the Middle East no doubt forget (if they ever knew) that in several situations (for example in Egypt and Syria), the Muslim armies were welcomed as liberators from the oppressive rule of Byzantium. Their memories tend to focus on the feeling that their ancestors lived for centuries as second-class citizens under Muslim rule, facing the burden of taxation and other restrictions summed up in the Covenant of Umar.[8] They cannot forget the Muslim rulers like al-Hakim who were particularly oppressive, or the occasions when the passions of the mob led to bloodshed. Remembering that over a period of around three centuries many of their ancestors renounced their Christian faith to become Muslims, they inevitably wonder whether it was the weakness of the churches, the attractions of Islam or sheer expediency which led them to accept the religion of their conquerors. Whatever their motives, their conversion created a situation in which the Christian community ceased to be the majority and became a minority under Islam. However much the historians remind us that Christian memories do not tell the whole story, this is part of the history which needs to be taken seriously, if only because of the way it still colours the attitudes of Arab Christians towards Islam today.

(ii)   The Middle Ages

Christendom inevitably felt that Islam posed a military threat to Europe. Having entered Spain and France, the Muslim armies may well have ventured even further if they had not been checked by Charles Martel at Tours in AD 732. From then on Christians had to reckon with the fact that while the Muslims were equal to them on the military level, on the cultural level the Muslims were distinctly superior. The encounter in Spain typifies much of the complexity and ambiguity in these relationships. Four centuries of generally peaceful coexistence produced a genuine and rich cultural encounter, but ended with the Reconquista, when the church determined to eradicate Islam, and gave Muslims the choice between conversion to Christianity, expulsion or execution.

The general attitude of Christians in Europe towards Islam during the Middle Ages has been summed up in terms of fear and horror, both of which were largely the product of ignorance.[9] In spite of all the beliefs that they held in common with Muslims, Christians saw Islam as a threat and felt compelled to produce their intellectual defences against what seemed to them to be an anti-Christian heresy. In doing so they invented all kinds of absurd legends about the Prophet, and produced a thoroughly distorted image of Islam, which has been passed down from generation to generation and no doubt still plays an important role in Europe's folk memory of Islam.[10]

With the call of successive popes to the Crusades in order to remove the shame of Christian holy places being held by Islam, the general attitude of Christians turned to hope and triumph. Now at last, it was felt, Christendom might be able to turn the tables on Islam and defeat the Muslims in their own heartlands under the sign of the cross. The dreams of

Christendom were fuelled by an extraordinary mixture of
piety and worldliness. But the end result was nothing more
than 'the embittering of relations between Christians and
Muslims for many generations and a vast amount of misrepresentation and misunderstanding on both sides'.[11] The en-
during power of these memories is illustrated by the fact that
Muslims in recent years have seen the Gulf War and the
conflict in Bosnia as a continuation of these same Crusades.

In spite of all the antagonism at both the military and
theological levels, Muslim writers like Nasr and Ahmad are at
pains to emphasize the amount of genuine respect and tolerance that existed during these centuries, and the extent of
Europe's cultural debt to Islam:

> The two civilisations respected each other, even if enmity ex-
> isted among them on a certain plane. The two made their own
> arms and were more or less evenly matched on the military and
> political plane . . . If the West called Muslims 'heathens', it
> nevertheless respected Islamic civilisation to the extent of emu-
> lating much of its science and philosophy, art and architecture,
> literature and mystical symbols as well as some of its major
> institutions, such as colleges of education . . . Despite theologi-
> cal anathema cast against Islam and the Crusades that caused
> great death and destruction, mediaeval Europe looked with
> respect upon the only 'other' it knew, that is, Islam and its
> society and civilisation.[12]

> There is also a long and brilliant history of peaceful relationships,
> diplomatic cooperation, economic and trade relationships, trans-
> fers of technology and the cross-fertilization of ideas and cultural
> experiences. In this respect, both have enriched each other. Any
> objective balance sheet of historical influences during the first
> millennium would lead to the conclusion that Islam's contribu-
> tion to the development of Europe and other Western countries
> has been immense. To ignore this bright and brilliant tradition
> and concentrate only on the experience of clash and confrontation
> is neither fair to history nor helpful in promoting better relations
> in the future . . .[13]

(iii) Renaissance and Enlightenment

According to Nasr,

> Open hatred of Islam, both intellectual and theological, really
> began with the Renaissance, which also deplored its own
> mediaeval past . . . This was the period of humanism in the
> nonreligious sense of the term – anthropomorphism, opposition
> to the certitude brought about by faith, individualism based upon
> rebellion against all higher authority, and also Eurocentrism, all
> of which have characterized the Western world-view ever since.[14]

At the time of the Reformation, Protestants saw Islam alongside Roman Catholicism as embodiments of the Antichrist,
while Catholics saw in Islam many of the features they hated
most in Protestantism. Then, with the coming of the Enlightenment, the rationalists took their turn to denigrate Islam and
pour scorn on the Prophet. Voltaire, for example, thought of
Muhammad as a fanatic, and Renan believed that Islam was
totally closed to new ideas, science, progress and freedom.
Nasr notes that Muslims for their part were shocked at the way
their Scriptures were handled: 'The Quran was and continues
to be analysed and criticized in the West not as the verbatim
Word of God, as Muslims believe, but simply as a human
compilation to be rent asunder by rationalist and historicist
methods.'[15]

(iv) The Ottoman Empire

If, as we shall see, many Muslims still feel deeply scarred by
their experience of Western imperialism, it is only fair to
remind ourselves that Islam has had great empires of its own.
Akbar S. Ahmed in *Discovering Islam: making sense of Muslim
history and society* has a chapter on 'The Great Empires: Ottomans, Saffavids and Mughals'.[16] While the Mughals are significant in the context of our survey because of their encounter
with the British in India, the Ottomans are particularly important because of their subjugation of the Christian Balkans and
their relationship with Europe and the West.

Here was an Empire that lasted from 1300 to 1922, with its
highest point in the sixteenth century. At various times it
controlled the middle East and north Africa, much of the
Balkans and eastern Europe, and in 1529 and 1683 came close
to capturing Vienna. From this time onwards the Empire
began to decay and decline, becoming eventually 'the sick man
of Europe'. While the Ottomans were attempting to imitate the
West, the European powers were expanding their influence
through trade and treaties, and attempting to weaken the
power of the Empire. In commenting on the relationship between the Ottomans and Europe, Akbar Ahmed speaks of 'the
fascination for European ways' and 'the obsession with Christian Europe'. Europeans, however, perceived the Ottomans as
'the hammer of Islam'. Thus when Ataturk came to power in
1922, he 'succumbed to the European obsession' and in turning
Turkey into a secular state, he 'Europeanized Turkey's cultural, social and religious life'.[17] The resurgence of Islamic
political activity in Turkey in recent years, however, demonstrates the dilemma of a country which finds itself caught in
an uneasy position between Islam and the West.[18]

(v) Western imperialism

It is often hard for people in the West to realize that the vast
majority of the Muslim world was under Western colonial
rule for periods of between fifty and two hundred years.
Philip Hitti suggests that from the Muslim perspective, this
domination was 'more pernicious than earlier encounters
because it came in the guise of educational and religious
missions that sought to "civilize" the Muslims and liberate
them from Islam'. Western imperialism was perceived as
'part of an all-out campaign on the part of the West to root
out Islam'.[19]

While Muslims could continue to pray in their mosques, they
felt the invasion of the West particularly keenly in the areas of
education and law. Two separate education systems developed
side by side: the traditional system based on the local school
(*maktab*) and the college (*madrasa*), and the European style of

education with its emphasis on rational inquiry, science and technology. The introduction of European systems of law (especially British and French) meant that law codes in many countries were Westernized to a greater or lesser degree, and the areas defined by Islamic law became narrower. Throughout this process, the Muslim world suffered from what they felt was the typical imperialist attitude of condescension and superiority towards conquered, less enlightened people. They suffered an acute loss of identity, realizing that their conquerors viewed the world of Islam, in the words of Hourani, as 'a quaking jelly which would slip into the hands of the European powers without difficulty'.[20]

(vi) The post-independence experience

The painfulness of the colonial experience gave way to euphoria and optimism as one country after another achieved independence. Kenneth Cragg explains the special significance of independence for Muslim countries by relating it to the close link in Muslim thinking between politics and religion:

> For reasons built into its origins, Islam has always been a confidently political religion . . . Muslims, by definition, were never meant to be alien-ruled. Their state was an inseparable part of their religion . . . To have forfeited that ruling status was the sting, the disquiet, the misery, of nineteenth-century history across the Islamic world. By the same token, to have reversed that distressful pattern and ousted the alien empires was like coming home into authenticity . . . the recovered amalgam of faith and power within Islamic societies is almost everywhere complete. This renewed and effective politicization is the most important single fact of the new century.[21]

This survey, in spite of its brevity, should at least explain why, in Albert Hourani's words, 'all these processes have created and maintained an attitude of suspicion and hostility on both sides and still provide, if not a reason for enmity, at least a language in which it can express itself'.[22]

2. The potential for conflict or coexistence

(i) Muslim opposition to secularism

Nasr explains the fundamental divide between the world-views of Islam and secularism:

> Between the Islamic world and the secularist West there can be no deep harmony and accord, for there are no common transcendent principles between them . . . Islam . . . has always opposed severely any titanic and Promethean view of humanity and has emphasized man's humble state before the grandeur and majesty of the Divine, seeing him at once as the servant of God (*'abd Allah*) and His vicegerent (*khalifat Allah*) on earth.[23]

> The very existence of the Islamic world, which negates so many assumptions of the postmediaeval and modern Western world-view, such as individualism, secular humanism, and the superiority of human rights over divine rights and humanly devised laws over Divine Law, appears as a formidable challenge to a West that considers its own historical development as the only acceptable path to follow for all other peoples on the globe.[24]

> Were Islam to have simply surrendered to Western patterns of thinking and acting, as do so many Muslim modernists, there would have been no confrontation between the two worlds.[25]

Nasr recognizes that 'much of the dialogue carried out between Christians and Muslims today is coloured by the presence of that silent third partner: anti-religious secularism'.[26]

(ii) Modern forms of Western domination

Nasr draws attention to the continuing economic domination of the West over the Muslim world: 'Many nations in the West not only control the most important economic asset of much of the Islamic world – oil – but also want in a thousand and one ways to recover the money they have paid for it, whether through the sale of arms or the creation of safe markets.'[27]

Along with economic domination there is 'the pressure for complete cultural domination':

> It is in the light of this whole lack of parallelism and complete inequality on the material plane, in which the West dictates, more or less, the agendas of the Islamic countries and judges them only on the basis of the extent to which they accept passing Western norms, now called, euphemistically, 'global', that the present relation between Islam and the West must be viewed. Many new elements have arisen of late, including the revival of Islam within the Islamic world and the pressure of the West for complete cultural domination . . .[28]

> Tapes of the Qur'an are not about to invade the airwaves of Europe and the United States as the crudest products of Western pop culture are invading the East, while Western secularism is seeking in a virulently aggressive manner to impose not only its technology, but also its half-dying worldview, through that technology, upon the non-Western world, especially the Islamic.[29]

He sees no hope of understanding between Islam and the West unless the West realizes how its arrogant and superior attitudes and behaviour are perceived:

> There is no possibility of creating understanding between the West and the Islamic world until, on the Western side, people realize that the very absolutisation of the West's particular world-view at the particular moment in time, when combined with powerful economic 'interests' that are usually against the interests of others, brings about impatience with and even hatred of other worldviews.[30]

Khurshid Ahmad similarly speaks of the possibility of 'a new colonial era' following the ending of the Cold War. The 'transition from colonial to post-colonial status' means that in a variety of ways the Muslim world remains very dependent on the West:

> The balance of power has so changed that the world is drifting towards a state of affairs where there may be only one super-

power, resulting in a new world order characterized by the political hegemony of that superpower over the rest, and giving rise to apprehensions among the smaller countries of the world about the beginning of a new colonial era.[31]

The last 300 years have been years of domestic and internal weakness as well as external domination for the Muslims. It is only during the last 50 years that Muslim countries have again emerged as independent states on the world political map. From the 1970s their relative economic position has improved, yet most Muslim countries remain economically underdeveloped and very much dependent upon the West, particularly for technology, capital and know-how. Politically, Muslim countries remain divided and unable to achieve a modicum of political unity and economic solidarity. By and large these countries are passing through a period of transition from colonial to post-colonial status. They are also facing a moral and cultural crisis. Moreover, the political influence, if not interference, of the West remains at a high watermark. A major concern of the emerging forces of Islamic resurgence relates to the degree of political, economic and cultural dependence of the Muslims on the Western world.[32]

Akbar Ahmed is particularly conscious of the pervasive influence of the media:

Nothing in history has threatened Muslims like the western media; neither gunpowder in the middle ages, which Muslims used with skill (recall Babar on the fields of Panipat winning India for his Mughal dynasty), nor trains and the telephone in the last century, which helped colonize them, nor even planes earlier this century (which they mastered for their national airlines). The western media are everywhere and present all the time; never resting and never allowing respite. They probe and attack ceaselessly, showing no mercy for weakness or frailty.[33]

(iii) The crisis within the West

Having heard the West boasting proudly about all that science, reason and freedom have achieved for the world, Muslims now hear the radical doubt and scepticism that seem to be eating away at the heart of the Western world-view and see plentiful evidence of social unrest and decay in the West. Nasr, for example, recognizes that 'the Renaissance paradigm, which has dictated the modern Western view of things, is itself falling apart along (with) the ever-increasing social chaos'.[34] While he acknowledges that 'in the West there is less political fighting today after several centuries of bloody revolutions and upheavals,' he is only too aware that 'there is also the deepest struggle and almost revolution on the question of values and ethics, not to speak of theology itself'.[35] What is to happen, therefore, if the foundations of secularism are being undermined? What does it mean for its engagement with Islam if the West is now caught up in a crisis of this kind?

(iv) The perceived threat of Islam

Ahmad explains how he believes Islam has come to be seen as a threat to the Western world:

> There is . . . a conspicuous search for new 'demons', 'threats', and 'evil empires' that may be made targets of attack so as to keep the political and economic power of the West solidified. In this respect, a rather systematic effort has been made for almost over a decade to project Islam and the Muslim world as one of those new threats. Even the tragic genocide of the Muslims in Bosnia is being justified, by some, as an effort 'to protect Europe from a fundamentalist Muslim State.' Even academics of repute have gone to the extent of seeing this tragic situation as an aspect of the current and more serious emerging 'Clash of Civilizations'. A number of intellectuals, scholars, journalists, political analysts, statesmen, and lobbyists are, in their own ways, trying to project Islam and the values it stands for as the 'new threat' to the West.[36]

He is disarmingly frank about what he sees as 'the political, economic, scientific, technological and military weakness of the Muslim world':

> As far as the military power and political strength of the Muslim world are concerned, they are weak and dependent on the West.

Where is the question of a military threat from the Muslim world? In the economic field, although rich in resources, the Muslim world's economic power has been marginalized and hardly has any economic leverage worth the name. There is also no reason to be obsessed with economic rivalries and the clash of commercial interests . . . it is through healthy competition and cooperation that the two can achieve the best economic results. In the fields of science and technology the West is far ahead of the Muslim world. Here again, through cooperation and competition, both stand to gain. In the fields of ideas, thought, information and communications, the West remains the pace-setter. Current revolutions in information technology and communication systems have opened up new possibilities for global cooperation, although the present disparity in control over these technologies also gives rise to certain apprehensions about 'cultural imperialism' . . . Whatever the efforts on the part of Muslims to make up for their weaknesses, it is the West which remains dominant, not the Muslim world.[37]

Nasr dismisses the language about the 'threat of Islam' just as emphatically as Ahmad, and points out that if anyone has reason to feel threatened, it is the Muslim world:

There is no common measure between the threats that the modern West poses for the whole existence of Islam and its civilisation and the threats, in reality and not as propaganda carried out by some of the media, that Islam poses for the West . . . the Islamic world cannot and does not threaten the West militarily, politically, or even economically in any conceivable way. On the contrary, the West controls the most vital economic resources of Muslim nations, benefits from all conflicts in that world through the sale of vast quantities of arms, and practically dictates its wishes in many parts of the Islamic world.[38]

(v)   Christianity and Judaism in the West

Nasr recognizes the fact that Christianity and Judaism are still alive in the West:

It is true that modernism has marginalised Christianity to an ever-greater degree since the Renaissance. Yet Christianity, as well as Judaism in the West, continue to survive as living realities . . . Muslims . . . must . . . remember that, although the West is predominantly secular, there has survived in the West to this day important Christian and also Jewish elements whose worldviews, despite transient worldly interests in some quarters, are close to that of Islam.[39]

He expresses his surprise at the way Christians seem to be prepared to change their fundamental beliefs:

From the Islamic point of view, what is difficult to understand is how various tenets of Christianity are changing so rapidly to the extent that some want to change the name and gender of Christ, whom they now call Christa. When modernism began, Christianity, especially in its Roman Catholic form, stood as the critic and opponent of modernism, whereas now many voices in the churches have become accomplices to the spread of the very ideas that have opposed the most fundamental tenets of the authentic Christian faith. The result is the constant change of even basic elements of the faith, so that it is difficult to understand with whom one is dialoguing.[40]

(vi) Muslim minorities in the West

Zaki Badawi, President of the Muslim College in London, describes the strange situation in which Muslims find themselves as a minority living under non-Muslim rule in the West, and the theological and practical dilemmas this poses for them:

As we know, the history of Islam as a faith is also the history of a state and a community of believers living by Divine law. The Muslims, jurists and theologians, have always expounded Islam as both a Government and a faith. This reflects the historical fact that Muslims, from the start, lived under their own law. Muslim theologians naturally produced a theology with this in view – it is a theology of the majority. Being a minority was not seriously

considered or even contemplated. The theologians were divided
in their attitude to the question of minority status. Some declared
that it should not take place; that is to say that a Muslim is
forbidden to live for any lengthy period under non-Muslim rule.
Others suggested that a Muslim living under non-Muslim rule is
under no obligation to follow the law of Islam in matters of public
law. Neither of these two extremes is satisfactory. Throughout the
history of Islam some pockets of Muslims lived under the sway
of non-Muslim rulers, often without an alternative. They none-
theless felt sufficiently committed to their faith to attempt to
regulate their lives in accordance with its rules and regulations in
so far as their circumstances permitted. In other words, the
practice of the community rather than the theories of the theologians provided a solution. Nevertheless Muslim theology offers,
up to the present, no systematic formulation of the status of being
a minority. The question is being examined. It is hoped that the
matter will be brought into focus and that Muslim theologians
from all over the Muslim world will delve into this thorny subject
to allay the conscience of the many Muslims living in the West
and also to chart a course for Islamic survival, even revival, in a
secular society.[41]

(vii)   Christian attitudes to Islam

While Christians have pronounced anathemas against Islam
in the past because it denies some of the most fundamental
Christian beliefs, they have had to recognize that it is at least
superior to paganism. In trying to understand the possible role
that Islam might be playing in the economy of God, they have
at times seen it as an instrument of divine judgment on the
church, and at others seen it as a genuine source of salvation.
Nasr, like many Muslims, finds real difficulty in the reluctance
of Christians to accept the authenticity of Muhammad, and
makes a strong plea for 'mutual acceptance':

> Few Christians accept Islam as an authentic religion or revelation
> and the Prophet as the receiver of a major message from Heaven
> coming after Christ. There is much diplomatic courtesy, but little

theological acceptance, especially by more traditional and conservative elements of Christianity ... Granted, accepting the authenticity of Islam is more difficult for Christianity than the acceptance of the authenticity of Christianity is for Islam, which, while denying the Trinity and Incarnation, accepts the divine origin of the Christian message and considers Christ as the supreme prophet of inwardness preceding the Prophet of Islam. Nevertheless, the question of mutual acceptance must be faced squarely.[42]

He sees Christian missionary activity, 'not as it was practised in the days of old, but as it has been practised by Western Christian missionaries since the colonial period and to this day', as a major obstacle to Muslim–Christian understanding:

Both Christianity and Islam are travelling religions that claim to be global messages, and neither religion can demand from the other that it discontinue 'preaching unto nations.' In the days of old, the material power behind the religious message of the two religions was more or less the same, in total contrast to what one observes today, where Western Christian missionary activity in the Islamic world is accompanied often, but not always, by enticement of the most worldly kind, usually relying upon the products of the very civilisation that has marginalised Christianity. There is usually the Bible in one hand and syringes or sacks of rice in the other, along with a schooling system that is more successful in secularising than Christianising its students ... in many areas missionary activity continues to be the instrument of Western secular interests, as it was during the colonial period ...

It is interesting to note in this context that Eastern Christians have not usually displayed such zeal as Western Christians, whose aggressive missionary spirit is due not only to Christianity but also to the Graeco-Roman civilisations, for which everyone other than themselves was a barbarian.[43]

(viii)   Muslim attitudes to Christianity

William Montgomery Watt explains the common Muslim belief in the self-sufficiency of Islam (the idea that Muslims have

nothing to learn from non-Islamic sources) by recounting a
story from early Islamic history which is 'almost certainly not
historically true but is yet significant':

> When in 642 the Muslims occupied Alexandria, the capital of
> Egypt and a leading centre of Hellenistic culture, they found the
> great library. The general in command wrote to the Caliph asking
> what was to be done with the books in the library and received
> the reply, 'If these books agree with the Qur'an, they are unnec-
> essary and may be destroyed; if they disagree with the Qur'an
> they are dangerous and should certainly be destroyed'. In other
> words, the Qur'an – and the Qur'an alone – has all the religious
> and moral truth required by all mankind until the Day of Judge-
> ment. In accordance with this feeling or assumption, Muslims
> have often avoided studying Christian, Western and other 'for-
> eign' books, or have borrowed from them without admitting it.[44]

During the lifetime of Muhammad, Muslims were genuinely
surprised by the fact that Christians and Jews did not recognize
him as a prophet, and Muslims to this day remain puzzled by
the reluctance of Christians to acknowledge Muhammad's
prophethood. Nasr encourages Muslims to try to see the problem from the Christian point of view:

> Muslims, often wary of ecumenical discussions because of their
> subsequent results and effects, must realize how difficult the task
> of acceptance of Islam as an authentic revelation is for a serious
> Christian theologian and not simply castigate the Christian be-
> cause he/she cannot accept the authenticity of the Islamic revela-
> tion as easily as can Islam the revelations of Judaism and
> Christianity.[45]

In spite of this he expresses the hope that Christians will
overcome their antagonism towards Muslim beliefs and recognize that they have more in common with Muslims than
with secular-minded Europeans:

> If one looks at the situation in depth, one sees that they (the
> Christians) have a great deal more in common with Muslims who

believe in God, accept the moral injunctions of the Ten Commandments, and seek to live a life centred upon prayer and the reality of the other world to which Christ referred in that most forgotten of his utterances, 'Seek ye first the Kingdom of God,' than with people whose mother tongue is English, French, German, or some other European language but who share nothing of the Christian worldview, whether it be of this world or the next. If a new awareness of this truth is to be created in the context of the present anti-Islamic current in the West . . . there would be a greater possibility for a serious accord between most of the Islamic world and, at least, *a* West if not what is called *the* West as defined by economic and geopolitical interests that are pursued at all costs, whether these 'interests' also accord with the interests of others or not.[46]

(ix) Major issues in Muslim eyes

Many Muslims feel that the West often betrays double standards, if not hypocrisy, in its judgments on other parts of the world. Its indignation seems to be very selective and determined largely by its own interests. Nasr, for example, draws attention to some of 'the real issues of basic importance in Muslim eyes': the loss of Muslim lands (especially in Palestine) and Western control of economic assets in the Muslim world, Bosnia and Chechenya. He explains some so-called 'Islamic' terrorism in terms of 'desperation before the forces that are destroying one's religion and civilisation'.[47]

Similarly Khurshid Ahmad speaks of the 'estrangement, even bitterness, so rampant amongst Muslims about Western attitudes, policies and strategies'.[48] He devotes several pages to his understanding of these major concerns for Muslims. His main points are these:

1. There is a general feeling among Muslims that Islam remains the most misunderstood religion in the West, not merely because of a lack of information but also because of a long tradition of misrepresentation and distortion . . .
2. Muslims also feel that there is a contradiction in the way some Western countries deal with Muslims as distinct from others.

For example, Israeli terrorism and violence are condoned, but Palestinian reaction is condemned as violence, pure and simple . . .

3. Muslims also feel that the West has little understanding of the real aspirations of Muslim peoples . . .
4. The way in which the forces of Zionism, born and nurtured in the West, are protected, promoted and strengthened and the way the people of Palestine are deprived of their homes and hearths is a further obstacle . . .
5. The manner in which Bosnia–Herzegovina was not allowed to continue on the political map despite the fact that the country came into existence through a democratic referendum and was recognized by both the UN and the European Community, which also gave assurances of protection of borders under international law is another irritant . . .
6. Although in the West there is a general acceptance of the plurality of political parties and actions, there is an implicit as well as explicit intolerance towards other cultures and religions . . .
7. The question of technology transfer and the extent of selectiveness and arbitrariness in this respect also intrigue the Muslims . . .
8. The West has also shown a great obsession with its own models of economic development and political democracy. Its efforts to make others follow this Western model and its unpreparedness to accept the position of others to discover their own paths to development and democracy remains enigmatic . . .[49]

(x) Muslim attitudes to the West

Khurshid Ahmad recognizes that not all Muslims respond to the West in the same way, and distinguishes three major trends in the Muslim world:

1. One dominant trend is represented by people who would like to align Muslim countries with the West, assimilate Western culture and values and in the name of 'modernization' opt for

'Westernization' without openly and completely discarding an Islamic nomenclature . . .

2. Second, there are forces representing the orthodox tradition, who would like to reject whatever comes from the West. Their main object is to protect and preserve whatever has come through tradition, even if Muslim countries have to be cut off from the stream of modern life . . .

3. There is however, a third and very powerful emerging trend which can rightly be described, not merely as a political phenomenon, or 'militant Islam', as some outsiders have chosen to describe it, but as a movement of cultural resurgence in the widest sense of the word. This movement stands for affirming Islamic identity and values and principles, social ideals and traditions . . . [50]

Ahmad identifies himself with the third of these three movements.

Conclusion

Some of these issues will be explored in the following chapters. Is it possible, however, to draw any conclusions on the basis of such a brief survey? At the risk of over-simplification, Muslims and Christians might ask themselves whether they can accept the following propositions as a starting point for further dialogue about their history:

(a) While many Christians and Muslims have never thought of their faith as a missionary faith, many on both sides have felt and still feel that their faith is true in some ultimate sense and therefore have wanted to commend it to others. Both faiths have generally thought of themselves as 'missionary faiths' in some sense, the one spreading out from Jerusalem, the other from Medina and Mecca.

(b) Both Christians and Muslims have at different times taken to the sword both to defend themselves and their faith and to extend their power and influence. In spite of the significant differences between the lives of Jesus and Muhammad, the concept of 'Christendom' is quite close to the idea of 'the House of Islam'.

(c) Both Islam and the West have had their Empires. If we speak so easily of 'Western imperialism', we must also speak of 'Islamic imperialism'. Both the imperialists and those who have been at the receiving end of the imperialism need to be able to reflect on the positive as well as the negative aspects of their experiences.

(d) Relations between Christians and Muslims in the past and present have almost always been deeply coloured by the political and social contexts in which they have related to each other. Much has depended on which community happens to be the majority and which is the minority, and on who has the balance of power.

It needs to be understood that in reflecting on the legacy of history in this way, the intention is not to use history to score points against the other side. Part of the task of dialogue is for both the main parties to listen to each other's interpretation of history and to accept that their own interpretations may need to be revised in one way or another. As Khurshid Ahmad suggests, the objective in reflecting on history in this way is not 'condemning or condoning the past' but rather the 'mending of fences for the future'.[51]

Notes

[1] Albert Hourani, *Europe and the Middle East*, Macmillan, London, 1980, p. 4.
[2] Khurshid Ahmad, 'Islam and the West: confrontation or cooperation?' *Muslim World*, vol. LXXXV. no. 1–2, Jan–April 1995, p. 80.
[3] Akbar S. Ahmed, 'Muslim Education and the Impact of the Western Mass Media', *Muslim Education Quarterly*, vol. 11, no. 3, 1994, The Islamic Academy, Cambridge, UK, p. 31.
[4] Seyyed Hossein Nasr, 'Islam and the West: yesterday and today', *Q-News International*, no. 248–50, 27 Dec 1996–9 Jan 1997, p. 11.
[5] Ahmad, op. cit., p. 63.

[6] For an attempt to describe the history and faith of the two communities side by side see Hugh Goddard, *Christians and Muslims: From double standards to mutual understanding*, Curzon Press, Richmond, 1995.

[7] Ahmad, op. cit., p. 63.

[8] See my *Cross and Crescent: responding to the challenge of Islam*, Inter-Varsity Press, Leicester, 1995, pp. 284–6.

[9] For example in Albert Hourani, *Europe and the Middle East*, Macmillan, London, 1980; R.W. Southern, *Western Views of Islam in the Middle Ages*, Harvard University Press, Cambridge, Massachusetts, 1962; and Norman Daniel, *Islam and the West: the making of an image*, Edinburgh University Press, 1980.

[10] See especially Daniel, op. cit.

[11] Trevor Ling, *A History of Religion East and West*, Macmillan, London and Basingstoke, 1968, p. 302.

[12] Nasr, op. cit., p. 10.

[13] Ahmad, op. cit., p. 74.

[14] Nasr, op. cit., pp. 10–11.

[15] Ibid., p. 11.

[16] Akbar S. Ahmed, *Discovering Islam: making sense of Muslim history and society*, Routledge, London, 1988, pp. 65–89.

[17] Ibid., p. 69.

[18] See for example, 'Can this be the century's greatest man?', pp. 18–19, and 'Father of Turk (sic) Nationalism', p. 20., both articles in *Q-News International*, no. 279–280, Nov 1997, pp. 18–20. Note also Maya Taggi's account of a meeting with the Turkish author Orhan Pamuk: 'For Turkey, says Pamuk, this conflict between Westernisers and Islamicists is more in lifestyle than a debate. "Turkey decided to be Westernised 200 years ago, and it's still in the process. Most of the country's struggles are located around that . . ." ' in 'Satire is Sacred', *Guardian Weekly*, 23 Nov, 1997.

[19] Philip Hitti, *Islam and the West*, Van Nostrand, Princeton, 1962, p. 7.

[20] Hourani, op. cit., p. 355.

[21] Kenneth Cragg, *The Call of the Minaret*, Collins, London, 1986, pp. 6–8.

[22] Hourani, op. cit., p. 4.

[23] Nasr, op. cit., p. 11.

24 Ibid., p. 11.
25 Ibid., p. 12.
26 Ibid., p. 26.
27 Ibid., p. 12.
28 Ibid., p. 11.
29 Ibid., p. 12.
30 Ibid.
31 Ahmad, op. cit., pp. 65–6.
32 Ibid., p. 67.
33 Ahmed, op. cit., pp. 22–3.
34 Nasr, op. cit., p. 11.
35 Ibid., p. 10.
36 Ahmad, op. cit., pp. 66–7. Fred Halliday provides an excellent analysis of the language of 'threat' and 'confrontation' in *Islam and the Myth of Confrontation: Religion and Politics in the Middle East*, I.B. Tauris, London, 1995.
37 Ibid., p. 69. It remains to be seen whether the current confrontation between Iraq's Saddam Hussein and the United Nations over weapons inspections (as of February 1998) eventually proves the rule expounded by Ahmed (by underlining the dominance of the West), or turns out to be an exception to the rule (by posing a continuing military threat to the West).
38 Nasr, op. cit., pp. 11–12.
39 Ibid., p. 12.
40 Ibid., p. 41.
41 Zaki Badawi, *Islam in Britain*, Ta Ha Publishers, London, 1981, pp. 26–7.
42 Nasr, op. cit., p. 13.
43 Ibid., p. 41
44 William Montgomery Watt, 'Islam and the West', in *Islam in the Modern World*, Denis MacEoin and Ahmed Al-Shahi (eds), Croom Helm, London and Canberra, 1983, p. 3.
45 Nasr, op. cit., p. 13.
46 Ibid., pp. 12–13.
47 Ibid., p. 12.
48 Ahmad, op. cit., p. 75.
49 Ibid., pp. 75–80.
50 Ibid., pp. 67–8.
51 Ibid., p. 74.

Two

Islamic Mission in the Past:
Persuasion without Compulsion?

Introduction

Call unto the way of Thy Lord with wisdom and fair exhortation ... (Qur'an 16:125).

There is no compulsion in religion (Qur'an 2:256).

Fight against such of those who have been given the Scripture as believe not in Allah nor the Last Day, and forbid not that which Allah hath forbidden by His messenger, and follow not the religion of truth, until they pay the tribute readily, being brought low (Qur'an 9:29).

Over the centuries ... domination by an alien religion had a wearing effect on the churches ... Conversion was greatly advanced by the political and military predominance of the Muslims (Nehemia Levtzion)[1]

Anyone who has been told that 'Islam was spread by the sword' inevitably thinks of soldiers standing over conquered peoples with drawn swords in their hands, offering the simple choice between Islam or death. If these images have (as one hopes) been banished long ago from our minds, what has taken their place? How did it happen that within a hundred years of the Prophet's death the Islamic Empire stretched from Spain to the borders of China and India? And how was it that within three hundred years the majority of non-Muslims in these areas had accepted the religion of their conquerors and become part of a single Islamic society? Was it simply a process of persuasion by words? This chapter attempts to summarize how Islamic mission worked in practice, and how the process of conversion took place.

1. The conversion of Arabia

The nearest word in Islam to the Christian concept of mission is *da'wa*, meaning 'call' (i.e. calling or inviting people to accept the faith of Islam). The Qur'an contains a clear call to mission in verses like: 'Call unto the way of Thy Lord with wisdom and fair exhortation, and reason with them in the better way . . .' (Q. 16:125). At the same time Muslims frequently quote the verse 'There is no compulsion in religion' (Q. 2:256), or, as Mahmoud Ayoub translates it, 'Let there be no coercion in religion'[2], claiming that Muslims have been forbidden to use unfair pressure of any kind to persuade people to accept Islam. There are other verses in the Qur'an, however, which call for a more aggressive approach towards certain kinds of non-Muslims: 'Fight against such of those who have been given the Scripture as believe not in Allah nor the Last Day, and forbid not that which Allah hath forbidden by His messenger, and follow not the religion of truth, until they pay the tribute readily, being brought low' (9:29; cf 9:123).[3]

How then in practice did Muslims carry out the task of mission? According to the earliest *Life of the Prophet* by Ibn Ishaq (written before AD 770), missionaries were sent out to the tribes around Medina after returning from the conquest of Mecca in 630.[4] This by itself, however, cannot be the whole story. Montgomery Watt believes the earliest expansion of Islam out of Medina needs to be related to the Arabian practice of the raid, expedition or razzia, which he describes as 'almost a form of sport' among the nomads of the Arabian deserts, where 'the aim was usually to drive off the camels of some other tribe'[5]. He goes on to say:

> The whole history of Muhammad's ten years at Medina came to be regarded as a series of razzias . . . Thus a razzia might lead

to a weak group in the neighbourhood of Medina asking to be taken into 'the protection of God and his prophet'. In this way the Jihad in the way of God might lead to the adoption of Islam by those who had been attacked.[6]

Jews, Christians and members of certain other religious groups therefore became 'protected communities' (*dhimmis*) under Islamic rule. Pagan Arabs, however, with no recognized religion, had no such privileges and had to choose between accepting Islam, being expelled from their land or being put to death.

Muhammad gradually extended his power in Arabia through a series of alliances in which one tribe after another came under the protection of the new Islamic state in Medina. Simply in order to survive and to prevent neighbouring tribes entering into alliances with each other, the new Muslim community had to draw the tribes within Arabia into the Islamic federation. Their motives for expansion were primarily political, and only secondarily religious. In the words of Montgomery Watt,

> Since apart from alliances, every tribe was against every other tribe, a tribe had to be either for Muhammad or against him after his conquest of Mecca. Neutrality was impossible when his power could be felt in most parts of Arabia. The decision to be for Muhammad or against him was basically a political decision. The religious aspect came in because Muhammad insisted that those who wanted to become his allies must accept him as a prophet, and this involved becoming Muslims.[7]

2. Mission and conquest in the middle East

According to Ibn Ishaq, Muhammad sent messengers before his death to the rulers of Yemen, Abyssinia, Egypt, Byzantium and Persia, inviting them to accept the religion of Islam.[8] Even if this did actually happen, however, Islamic mission was probably not the main motive in the minds of the Muslims who ventured out of Arabia. 'The Islam that first conquered,' says Philip Hitti, 'was not the religion but the state, not Muhammadanism but

Arabianism. The Arabians burst upon an unsuspecting world as a nationalist theocracy seeking a fuller life.'[9] Watt suggests that the same dynamic operated for the expansion of Islam both inside and outside the Arabian peninsula:

> The Jihad of the first great expansion is a development of the Arabian razzia – a logical development because of the increasing extension of the *pax islamica*. Most of the participants in the expeditions probably thought of nothing more than booty – movable booty was distributed among them. Some of them were certainly pious Muslims to whom it meant something that they were fighting in the way of God. More of them probably believed that, if they died in the fighting, they would be reckoned martyrs and would go to Paradise. There was no thought of spreading the religion of Islam; apart from other considerations that would have meant sharing their privileges of booty and stipends with many neo-Muslims. It doubtless increased their self-esteem that the 'strong tribe' of Muslims should take under its protection the 'weak tribes' of Jews and Christians. The most that can be said at the level of the individual is that religious and materialistic motives support one another. At the level of the high command, however, the religious idea of the solidarity of all believers and its corollary of the necessity of directing warlike energies outwards led to the building of an empire. Muhammad cannot have foreseen the expansion in detail, but the fact that at his death, when the situation in Medina was threatening, Abu-Bakr did not cancel an expedition towards Syria, suggests that Muhammad had impressed on his lieutenants the centrality of the need for movement outwards.[10]

Whatever we think today of the *dhimma* system that brought Jewish and Christian communities under Islamic rule, we should recognize that it was considerably better than the system for minorities that operated within the Byzantine Empire, and far more enlightened than anything that Western Christendom could come up with for many centuries. Watt's evaluation of the status of Jews and Christians in the middle East in this earlier period probably represents the consensus of Western scholarship on the subject today:

In the early days of the Islamic empire the Christian inhabitants of Egypt and the Fertile Crescent were probably better off as *dhimmis* under Muslim Arab rulers than they had been under Byzantine Greeks. One of the reasons why the system worked well was that among the pre-Islamic Arabs it had been a matter of honour for the desert tribe to show that its protection was effective, and something of this attitude to the *dhimmis* passed to Muslim rulers. On the whole there was more genuine toleration of non-Muslims under Islam than there was of non-Christians in mediaeval Christian states. There were exceptions, of course. When times were hard and difficult, non-Muslims would tend to get the worst of it. Occasionally, too, a ruler, in order to divert animosity from himself, would encourage the mob to vent its feelings on the *dhimmis*. On the whole, however, the 'protected minorities' had a tolerable existence.[11]

3. The process of Islamization

When the Muslim Arab conquerors established themselves and their families as colonists all over the middle East in major centres like Damascus, Kufa and Basra, they were still a tiny minority ruling over populations in which the vast majority were non-Muslims. At this stage their Islamic faith, as Richard Bulliet points out in his book *Conversion to Islam in the Mediaeval Period*, was probably not 'the religion that is described in general books on Islam', but rather 'something far more primitive and undeveloped, a mere germ of later developments'. As a result, 'the society of these conquered lands was certainly not an Islamic one to begin with'.[12]

The local populations of Jews, Christians and Zoroastrians were offered protection of life and property by the new Muslim rulers. They paid the *jizya* tax, were given autonomy to run their own communities as they wished, and allowed to practise their own religion with comparative freedom. As trade and social contacts increased, however, there was a process of gradual conversion to Islam, which took place at different speeds in different areas. In Egypt, for example, very few Coptic Christians converted at the time of the Arab conquest in AD 642. It was only after 800 that they began to convert in larger numbers, and even after 900 the Copts were still a substantial minority. After 1300, during a period of increasing Muslim intolerance towards minorities, the Coptic community decreased to around its present proportion (between 7 and 10 per cent) of the total population.[13] In the rest of north Africa the Berber tribes accepted Islam, and many hundreds were recruited into the Arab army.[14] According to Muslim tradition, however, they apostasized twelve times before their final acceptance of Islam.[15] The general picture, therefore, seems to be that for most of the middle East, Syria and Iraq, 'the primary conversion process ... was essentially complete by 1010'.[16]

If we ask why so many Christians were open to change their religion, it is not hard to appreciate the cumulative effect of Islamic rule over Christian communities. In the words of Levtzion, 'over the centuries ... domination by an alien religion had a wearing effect on the churches; their property dwindled and the spiritual and moral standards of their clergy declined. Christian sources blamed the ignorance and corruption of the clergy for the defections of Christians in Syria and in Egypt, as well as in Asia Minor.'[17] Three major weaknesses in the churches seem to have been: doctrinal conflicts that were heavily influenced by the dominant cultures of Greece and Rome; weaknesses in the moral, social and political teaching of the churches; and folk Christianity without adequate teaching.

In the process of Islamization within the Empire it is possible to discern a pattern of five distinct stages: the formal confession of faith, social conversion, the creation of Islamic institutions, the creation of a single Islamic society, and finally reform.

(i)   The formal profession of faith

All that was necessary for an individual to accept Islam was the recital of the *shahada*, the basic creed of Islam: 'I bear witness that there is no god but God (Allah), and Muhammad is the Apostle of God.' In a book of essays entitled *Conversion to Islam in the Mediaeval Period*, edited by Nehemia Levtzion of the Hebrew University in Jerusalem, the editor points out that there was no rite of initiation comparable to baptism, and there was no need for a priest-like person to be present when the profession was made.[18] The situation in Asia Minor described by V.L. Menage could perhaps apply to other areas as well: 'It is doubtful whether any but a few converts received instruction in their new faith; for the great majority conversion entailed no more than the *shahada*, circumcision, new clothes, and perhaps a cheerful parade ...'[19] After the profession of faith no reversion to Judaism or Christianity was tolerated. Muslim men could marry non-Muslim women, and their children would of course be brought up as Muslims.[20]

(ii) Social conversion

Even more important than the formal profession of faith, however, was the process of joining the Muslim community. Instead of defining his identity in terms of tribe or nation, the convert from now on, says Bulliet, 'saw his identity in terms of the new religious community of which he had become a member'.[21] Sometimes this meant individuals moving to live alongside a larger Muslim community.[22] At other times whole communities converted, following their leaders or tribal chiefs.[23]

One significant feature in this early stage of the process was that many of the pressures to develop structures within the Islamic community came from the new converts who had come over from non-Christian religions. As Jews, Christians and Zoroastrians they had grown up with rabbis, priests, bishops and so on, who constituted formal authority structures, acted as spokesmen for their communities, and enjoyed a degree of legal autonomy which enabled them to deal with questions of personal status. In places like Kufa, Basra and Baghdad, a new phenomenon was coming into being – 'an urban mass society' in which the majority were Muslims. And these new Muslim communities had to develop their own ways of fulfilling all the social functions (rites of passage and the like) which had been met within the other religions. Many features of the newly developed Muslim communities therefore had an uncanny resemblance to those from which the new converts had come![24]

(iii) The creation of Islamic institutions

According to traditional Islamic political thought, when Muslim rule was established in a community, it automatically became part of *dar al-Islam*. After this 'a more or less uniform set of social and religious institutions' was established, the most important of which were the mosque, the Islamic school and the court.[25] Trading would come within an economic system regulated by Islamic practice. At a later stage, from around AD 1000, further institutions like the Sufi orders, Muslim brotherhoods and trade guilds became more and more important. The spread of these institutions created what Levtzion calls 'an Islamic ambience'.[26]

(iv) The creation of a single Islamic society

In this fourth stage of the process, according to Larry Poston in *Islamic Da'wah in the West: Muslim missionary activity and the dynamics of conversion to Islam*, 'Muslim control of these institutions (particularly the legislative and judicial branches of government) contributed to the progress of Islamization, even though these structures were not used to impose Islam *directly* upon the people.'[27] He goes on to explain that the purpose behind these developments was 'to gradually pervade the culture at all levels and thus make conversion more socially acceptable than it would have been had Islam remained a completely alien faith. In short, Muslims entered a society at its uppermost levels and extended their influence downward to the masses.'[28]

The resulting Muslim society is described by Levtzion as

A society in which Islam has achieved such a numerical preponderance in comparison with other religions that its social institutions determine the complexion of the society as a whole. This means not simply that Muslims are in the majority, but that their institutions have been adapted to a mass following, and alternative religious and institutional structures pertaining to minority religions are no longer seen as a potentially vital threat to Islam.[29]

Bulliet ends his study on *Conversion to Islam in the Mediaeval Period* with the telling observation that the single most significant factor in the process of Islamization was not the power of the governments or political leaders, but 'the emergence of a powerful and dynamic social and religious elite within the local Muslim community'.[30] This is particularly important for challenging the generalizations that are often made about the close identification between religion and state (*din* and *dawla*) in Islam. He concludes that in the period covered by his study 'the true central thread of Islamic history lies not in the political realm of the caliphs and sultans but in the social realm where the *ulama* (religious teachers) served as the functioning heart of the historic Muslim community'.[31]

(v) Reform

If the creation of an Islamic society could not ensure that every individual would follow the Muslim way of life, something further was needed to turn nominal Muslims into 'good Muslims' or 'better Muslims'. For, in the words of Levtzion, 'Islamization of a social or ethnic group is not a single act of conversion but a long process towards greater conformity and orthodoxy.'[32] In many situations, it was several centuries after the initial conversion to Islam that this process of reform took place. This need for reform can be seen most clearly in Arabia, the very heartland of Islam:

> The majority of the Arab tribesmen accepted Islam collectively, in what might be described as a passive adhesion to Islam. The significance of the religious change became evident only when they emerged from the Arabian Peninsula . . . Those tribes who remained behind in the wastes of the Arabian Peninsula maintained their previous way of life, which was not very different from that of the pre-Islamic period. For some of them a meaningful conversion to Islam was delayed perhaps until the rise of the Wahhabi reform movement [i.e. the eighteenth century].[33]

In other parts of the Muslim world, it was Sufis who played the most significant role in deepening people's understanding and practice of Islam. According to the Indian historian S.M. Ikram, 'The *sufis* were much happier when they helped one who was already a Muslim to become a better Muslim than when they saw a non-Muslim become a Muslim.'[34] In west Africa the *jihad* of 1804, according to Murray Last, 'was primarily a reform movement, reforming lax Muslims, not converting pagans. It was ideologically probably less concerned with the *kufr* [unbelief] of pagans than with the *kufr* of those Muslims who opposed the *jihad*.'[35] Without this process of reform the practice of Islam in many areas might have remained rather nominal.

4. The 'missionaries' of Islam

One of the first western scholars to challenge the popular view that 'Islam was spread by the sword' was T.W. Arnold, the author of *The Preaching of Islam: a history of the propagation of the Muslim faith*, first published in 1896. The main message of the book is summed up in the Introduction as follows:

> It is not in the cruelties of the persecutor or the fury of the fanatic that we should look for the evidence of the missionary spirit of Islam . . . but in the quiet, unobtrusive labours of the preacher and the trader who have carried their faith into every quarter of the globe.[36]

Arnold and other historians have helped us to see that when the Arab armies were establishing Islamic rule over north Africa and the middle East and parts of north India, it was not soldiers who were the main agents in proclaiming the message of Islam. In many other areas of the world outside the great Islamic Empires in the middle East and north Africa, armies played no part at all in spreading the message. The most significant 'missionaries' of Islam can be divided into three categories, as follows.

(i) Traders

After the initial spread of Islam in the Middle East and Africa through the Arab armies, it was traders who carried Islam beyond the borders of the Empire into central Asia as far as China, from Egypt and north Africa to sub-Saharan Africa, from the middle East to the coast of east Africa, and from India to Indonesia. The important connection between Islam and trade can perhaps best be traced back to Muhammad and the early situation in Mecca where, in the words of M. Shaban, 'trade and religion were inseparable, and no one could reject the one and expect to participate in the other'.[37] Levtzion suggests one reason why traders were likely to be more effective in spreading Islam: 'The mobility of the traders stands in stark contrast to the stability of the peasants. The latter are more strongly attached to local spirits and to the deities of nature, whereas traders are more susceptible to the adoption of a universal and abstract religion.'[38] Arnold paints this idyllic picture of the Muslim trader at work as a missionary:

> Wherever Islam has made its way, there is the Muhammadan missionary to be found bearing witness to its doctrines – the trader, be he Arab, Pul or Mandingo, who combines proselytism with the sale of his merchandise, and whose very profession brings him into close and immediate contact with those he would convert, and disarms any possible suspicion of sinister motives.[39]

(ii) Teachers

Levtzion explains how a variety of 'Muslim divines, professional men of religion' built on the work of the traders:

> Traders did open routes, expose isolated societies to external cultural influences, and maintain communications. But it seems that traders were not themselves engaged in the propagation of Islam. They were accompanied or followed by Muslim divines, professional men of religion, who rendered religious services to the traders in the caravans or to the newly established commercial communities. Some of these men were tempted to stay behind at the court of a chief who bought their services, and initiated the process of Islamization in that chiefdom.[40]

One of the first activities of any Muslim missionary in a new situation was to start teaching the Qur'an and the basics of

Islam. The importance of teaching is vividly illustrated by the following account, recorded by Arnold, of the instructions given to a group of Muslims who had been expelled from Spain in 1492 and were asked to go in parties of five or six to live among the tribes in a mountainous area in North Africa:

> It is a duty incumbent upon us to bear the torch of Islam into those regions that have lost their inheritance in the blessings of religion; for these unhappy Kabils are wholly unprovided with schools, and have no shaykh to teach their children the laws of morality and the virtues of Islam; so they live like the brute beasts, without God or religion. To do away with this unhappy state of things, I have determined to appeal to your religious zeal and enlightenment. Let not these mountaineers wallow any longer in their pitiable ignorance of the grand truths of our religion; go and breathe upon the dying fire of their faith and re-illumine its smouldering embers; purge them of whatever errors may still cling to them from their former belief in Christianity: make them understand that in the religion of our lord Muhammad . . . dirt is not, as in the Christian religion, looked upon as acceptable in the eyes of God . . . Go, my children, bearing the message of salvation, and may God be with you and uphold you.[41]

(iii)   Sufi holy men

Alongside the traders and teachers there were the charismatic figures who lived with people in the villages, meeting their personal needs and often engaging in a kind of 'power encounter'. 'Those people who spread Islam,' says Fazlur Rahman, 'were mainly Sufis who attracted non-Muslim masses towards Islam by their spiritual activity and their broad humanitarian services to all sorts of people whether Muslim or non-Muslim.'[42] Levtzion believes that the adaptability of Islam was a major factor in facilitating 'the peaceful process of Islamization': 'In its first encounter with people of other religions Islam was not presented in all its vigor (and prophetic exclusiveness). Its representatives, mainly popular divines, emphasized what was common to Islam and the local religions, using prayers, amulets, and other charms to recruit supernatural aid.'[43]

Speaking of the spread of Islam in India, Professor A.B.M. Habibullah writes: 'It is through such contacts, fostered by the simplicity and broad humanism of the *sufi*, that Islam obtained its largest number of free converts and it is in this sense that he is considered a missionary.'[44] Levtzion sums up the combined influence of the traders, teachers and holy men by saying: 'Muslims were considered to be superior because of their literacy, magical and healing efficacy, and their wealth.'[45]

5. The appeal of Islam

The most attractive features of Islam can be summarized as follows and illustrated by examples from a wide variety of situations.

(i) Liberation from oppressive foreign rule

A Christian tribe in the Jordan valley sent the following message to the Muslim army as it approached:

> O Muslims, we prefer you to the Byzantines, though they are of our own faith, because you keep better faith with us and are more merciful to us and refrain from doing us injustice and your rule over us is better than theirs, for they have robbed us of our goods and our homes.[46]

Egypt provides another clear example of Christian communities that welcomed the Muslim invaders because of the opportunity they offered to throw off the oppressive rule of Byzantium and its interference in their church affairs.[47] In Spain slaves and persecuted Jews were among the first converts to Islam.[48]

(ii) Improvement in social or economic status

During the early phase of expansion led by the Arab armies the majority of the first non-Arab converts were 'prisoners of war who might seek through conversion to escape slavery and people, such as poor farm laborers, from the very lowest classes'.[49] They were in general 'the dregs of society'.[50] Although they became in effect 'second-class Arabs', this new status must have been an improvement on their previous situation. When the imperial army of Iran was defeated, its cavalry officers converted to Islam and joined the Muslim army, receiving more pay than they had previously received.[51] Similarly when some of the landed aristocracy in Iran converted, they were exempted from the poll tax.[52]

A similar dynamic was no doubt at work in the later Middle Ages, when during periods of distress, 'people converted to escape humiliating conditions. In some extreme situations, in an atmosphere of religious fanaticism, non-Muslims were subject to physical assaults by the masses, to official persecution, and to forced conversions.'[53] In the Ottoman Empire and Mughal India there are examples of fief holders 'who may have adopted Islam in order to hold on to their offices and property or in order to secure official forbearance after they had failed to pay their dues to the treasury'.[54] In India Islam was often attractive to Hindus because it offered release from the caste system.[55]

(iii) Success

The successfulness of the initial conquests and the spread of the faith at later stages would have been seen by many as evidence that God was on the side of Islam. So, for example, in a study on the theme of conversion in Swahili literature in east Africa, Jan Knappert writes that 'Islam had the prestige of the successful men's religion'. The victories of Muhammad and his successors were a major theme in Swahili literature, and demonstrated how 'success is Islam's advertisement'.[56] Knappert also suggests that in the African context it was natural for people to make the connection between the success of Muslims in business and their amulets.[57]

(iv) Supernatural power

Christians today have to reckon with the fact that many phenomena which they understand in terms of 'power encounter' have been reported in the context of other faiths. In Indonesia, for example, one recurring feature in the myths explaining the conversion of different rulers is 'the influence of some supernatural event'.[58] In India there are stories of 'tournaments in magical powers between *jogis* and *sufis*', where the defeat of the *jogis* is followed by the group's acceptance of Islam.[59] Similarly Arnold describes how an Indian raja set up a series of tests to decide between the competing claims of the local Hindus and a group of Muslims who settled beside the Hindu temple:

> As a final test, he had them both tied up in sacks filled with lime and thrown into tanks. The Hindu priest never reappeared, but Baba Fakhr al-Din asserted the superiority of his faith by being miraculously transported to a hill outside the town. The Raja hereupon became a Musalman, and his example was followed by a large number of the inhabitants of the neighbourhood, and the temple was turned into a mosque.[60]

Levtzion records the story of a chief/king of Malal in Senegal who after many years of drought was encouraged by a Muslim to accept Islam and immediately found that his prayers for rain were answered. He concludes: 'This Muslim succeeded in winning over the king by demonstrating the omnipotence of Allah, praying to Allah having saved the kingdom where all sacrifices by local priests had failed. Islam made its earliest appeal in competition with the African traditional religions, proving its superiority as a source of blessings.'[61]

(v) Tolerant spirit

In the agreement made with the people of Jerusalem when it was captured in AD 636, Umar guaranteed to the Christians 'security for their lives, their possessions, their churches and their crosses, and for all that concerns their religion'. Their churches would not be destroyed or turned into dwelling places.[62] T.W. Arnold believed that in Spain 'it was probably in a great measure their tolerant attitude towards the Christian religion that facilitated their rapid acquisition of the country.[63]

During the Crusades many of the Christians of Palestine preferred to be ruled by Muslims than by the Crusaders.[64] Similarly Serbian Orthodox Christians at one time preferred to be ruled by Muslims than by Roman Catholics from Hungary.[65] It was not only Christians who were impressed by the tolerance of Muslims. In the Sind, which was at one time largely Buddhist, the tolerance of the Arabs seems to have won over many Buddhists towards Islam.[66]

(vi)   Closeness to the Christian faith

In many situations it would have been the similarities between the two faiths that commended Islam to Christians. Writing about conversion in the medieval period, Richard Bulliet suggests that as a general principle people often convert 'more for mundane than for spiritual reasons'. When they are 'more or less satisfied with their previous religious life' and then accept a new religion, it is likely that they 'find life in the new religion more attractive the closer it approximates life in the old'.[67]

A heretical Christian sect in Bosnia known as Bogomiles provides an example of this principle at work. When persecuted by the Roman Catholic Church, they appealed to the Turks to protect them from the king of Bosnia, and later embraced Islam in large numbers after the Turkish conquest.[68] Some of their beliefs and practices were very close to those of Islam: they believed that Christ was not crucified; they rejected the worship of Mary, baptism and priesthood, the use of crosses, images and relics, bells, and the drinking of wine; and their churches were simple and unadorned.

(vii)   Cultural accommodation

While some pagan practices have been condemned, and idols and fetishes destroyed, the spread of Islam has generally been accompanied by a minimum of cultural dislocation, and the underlying primal or folk religion has not always been challenged or radically transformed. Thus in rural districts of Asia Minor Islam spread relatively easily among ill-instructed Christians, because, in the words of Menage, 'an Islam already diluted by the tolerance of pagan Turkish beliefs and customs became still further diluted by the adoption as popular cult-centers of the Christian (and pre-Christian) sacred sites – tombs, springs, trees etc – and the accretion of Christian feast days, saints, and even ritual.'[69] Levtzion argues that 'the Islamization of Africa became more successful because of the Africanization of Islam.'[70]

He also believes that even in places as different as Indonesia and Morocco, west Africa and India, 'Islam was so assimilated into the local cultures as to be considered an indigenous religion. Diversity, however, did not break the unity of Islam, and the many local forms should be considered as variations of one universal religion.'[71] He points to Java as an example of Islam's ability to adapt – in this case to an underlying mysticism:

> Javanese Islam was mystical, a natural development given the predominantly mystical thrust of previous religions in Java. Being by nature committed to mysticism, Javanese Muslims were relatively unconcerned with personal practice. Islam became the religion of nearly all the Javanese largely because it adapted successfully to the main configurations of preexisting Javanese religions. It gave greater richness to Javanese religion without requiring the abandonment of older ideas . . . It did not fundamentally alter the mystical theme; it gave it yet another vocabulary, a new range of explanations and illustrations, a new set of powerful ritual phrases. And it was tolerant . . . Thus Java came to be a Muslim society, but one in which Islam was only a part of the vast cultural heritage.[72]

The following account, written in Nigeria in 1911, represents a Christian interpretation of how the process of conversion to Islam worked out in practice:

> Islam, despite its shortcomings, does not, from the Nigerian point of view, demand race suicide of the Nigerian as an accompaniment of conversion. It does not stipulate revolutionary changes in social life, impossible at the present stage of Nigerian development; nor does it undermine family or communal authority. Between the converter and converted there is no abyss. Both are

equal, not in theory, but in practice, before God. Both are African;
sons of the soil. The doctrine of the brotherhood of man is carried
out in practice. Conversion does not mean for the converted a
break with his interests, his family, his social life, his respect for
the authority of his natural rulers.[73]

(viii)   Simplicity and rationality

In the area of morality, Islam has frequently been presented as
a religion that does not make unreasonable ethical demands.
Thus Arnold, for example, singles out the strong appeal of
different concepts of holiness and sexual morality in Islam: 'A
theory of the Christian life that found its highest expression in
asceticism of the grossest type could offer little attraction in the
face of the more human morality of Islam.'[74] This general idea
is further illustrated by Jan Knappert's study of conversion in
Swahili literature, where in the African context virility is seen
as an argument for Islam:

> Virility is apparently used as an argument for Islam . . . one may
> infer that the argument is not lost on African men. Contrast this
> with the Christian preaching for abstemious behavior, the im-
> plied ideal of celibacy in Christian thinking ('No wife is better
> than one, but one is permitted to prevent sin'), literally quoted
> from an Islamic preacher in East Africa. Swahili oral traditions,
> however, state explicitly that four wives are better than one, since
> man must rule and one wife might think that she is her husband's
> equal.[75]

Christians who found difficulty with concepts like trinity,
incarnation and atonement would inevitably be attracted by
the short and simple creed of Islam: 'I bear witness that there
is no god but God, and Muhammad is the Apostle of God.'
In the African context, according to Levtzion, 'initial demands
on the new Muslim were minimal. Only after Islam had gained
a foothold in a society did the exclusive nature of this prophetic
religion gradually become manifest.'[76] The contrast between
the complexity of Christian doctrine and the rationality of
Islam is highlighted in this revealing conversation of a Coptic

Christian with a Muslim, as recorded by a Muslim writer in the eleventh century:

> My proof for the truth of Christianity is, that I find its teachings contradictory and mutually destructive, for they are repugnant to reason and revolting to the intellect, on account of their inconsistency and mutual contrariety. No reflection can strengthen them, no discussion can prove them; and however thoughtfully we may investigate them, neither the intellect nor the senses can provide us with any argument in support of them. Notwithstanding this, I have seen that many nations and mighty kings of learning and sound judgment have given their allegiance to the Christian faith; so I conclude that if these have accepted it in spite of all the contradictions referred to, it is because the proofs they have received, in the form of signs and miracles, have compelled them to submit to it.[77]

(ix)   Moral superiority

Some words written in 1688 and quoted by Arnold no doubt express the feelings of many Christians who have come in contact with devout, practising Muslims:

> If Christians will but diligently read and observe the Laws and Histories of the Mahometans, they may blush to see how zealous they are in the works of devotion, piety, and charity, how devout, cleanly, and reverent in their Mosques, how obedient to their Priest, that even the great Turk himself will attempt nothing without consulting his Mufti; how careful are they to observe their hours of prayer five times a day wherever they are, or however employed; how constantly do they observe their Fasts from morning till night a whole month together; how loving and charitable the Muselmans are to each other, and how careful of strangers may be seen by their Hospitals, both for the Poor and for Travelers; if we observe their Justice, Temperance, and other moral Virtues, we may truly blush at our own coldness, both in devotion and charity, at our injustice, intemperance, and oppression; doubtless these Men will rise up in judgment against us; and surely their devotion, piety and works of mercy are main causes of the growth of Mahometism.[78]

A European traveller in Ethiopia in the nineteenth century observed that Muslims were regarded as being much more honest, trustworthy and energetic than Christians, and were therefore favoured in employment. Every Muslim ensured that his sons were taught to read and write, whereas Christians were educated only when they were intended for the priesthood.[79] Arnold comments that 'this moral superiority of the Muhammadans of Abyssinia over the Christian population goes far to explain the continuous though slow progress made by Islam during the eighteenth and nineteenth centuries.'[80]

(x) Culture and civilization

It may be hard for people from the West to appreciate that for many centuries the world of Islam was perceived to be more powerful than Europe. Its achievements in literature, medicine, mathematics, astronomy and engineering must have given many a sense of cultural inferiority. The Christians of Spain, for example, would have seen the attraction of a religion which had so much more to offer in terms of learning and science than their own at that time:

> The majority of the converts were no doubt won over by the imposing influence of the faith of Islam itself, presented to them as it was with all the glamour of a brilliant civilization, having a poetry, a philosophy and an art well calculated to attract the reason and dazzle the imagination: while in the lofty chivalry of the Arabs there was free scope for the exhibition of manly prowess and knightly virtues – a career closed to the conquered Spaniards that remained true to the Christian faith. Again, the learning and literature of the Christians must have appeared very poor and meagre when compared with that of the Muslims, the study of which may well by itself have served as an incentive to the adoption of their religion.[81]

6. The question of 'forcible conversion'

We have already seen that the process of Islamization created the context in which it was easy and natural for Jews and

Christians in particular to accept the faith of Islam. But were there deliberate attempts to persuade them to convert? And was there any use of force? The majority of historians tell us that most of the time there was no deliberate policy of encouraging Jews and Christians to convert to Islam. 'Practically,' says Mohamed Talbi, 'Islam itself was never imposed by compulsion.'[82] Historians point out that the continued existence of Christian communities in the middle East until the present day is evidence of the toleration extended to these minorities. If there had been a fixed policy of forced conversion or expulsion (as there was in England when the Jews were expelled, or in Spain when the Muslims were expelled during the Reconquista), it is unlikely that any Christian communities would have survived.[83]

There are, however, a number of examples of forced conversion from different areas and at different periods of history. In his study of the process of Islamization in Asia Minor, V.L. Menage concludes that there must be some basis in fact to the stories of forced conversion and martyrdom in the churches in Asia Minor, even if 'the duress implied by the term "forcible conversion" might be something less immediate than a dagger at the throat'.[84] One obvious example in this area is the system of *devshirme* in the Ottoman Empire, whereby boys were recruited by force from the *dhimmi* communities to be trained to serve in the Ottoman administration and army during the fifteenth and sixteenth centuries.[85]

Even Sir Thomas Arnold, with his emphasis on the peaceful spread of Islam, in surveying the evidence from India, was forced to admit that 'it is established without doubt that forced conversions have been made by Muhammadan rulers in India'.[86] Peter Hardy in a more recent study gives examples from Malabar, Bengal, Sind, the north-west provinces and the Punjab, Delhi and Agra. And he concludes his study of conversion to Islam in India by saying that 'a majority of European commentators . . . has accepted that some conversions by the use of force did occur'.[87] In assessing the evidence from a wide variety of places and times Levtzion concludes: 'Although it is difficult to assess the relative importance of forced conversions in the general process of Islamization, they seem to have weighed less than is implied in non-Muslim sources and more than is admitted by Muslims.'[88]

A second valuable source of evidence in this debate is the commentaries on the Qur'anic texts quoted earlier about freedom and compulsion in religion (2:256 and 9:29). Muslim commentators, according to Vardit Rispler-Chaim, were wrestling with two problems concerning freedom of religious belief: firstly, how to reconcile the verse condemning the use of coercion with those calling for warfare, and secondly, how to reconcile the theory and ideals presented in the Qur'an with the realities of what had actually happened in the history of Islam.

She gives the following as examples of precedents that were recorded by the commentators and interpreted as demonstrating that compulsory conversion was *prohibited* by Muhammad and his immediate followers:

> A Muslim named Al-Husayn had two sons, who having been influenced by Christian merchants, converted to Christianity and left Medina to go to Syria with these missionary merchants. Al-Husayn pleaded with the Prophet to pursue the convoy and bring his sons back to Islam. But the Prophet once again said 'there is no compulsion in religion', that is, let them follow the religion of their choice, even though it is not Islam.
>
> The Caliph Umar proposed to his Christian servant, Asbaq, that he adopt Islam. When the latter refused, Umar simply explained to him that as a Muslim he could bring more benefit to other Muslims, through marriage and participation in *jihad*, etc. than as a Christian. Umar did not impose Islam on a servant despite the fact that in those days servants, being part of their property, could be compelled to adopt their master's religion.[89]

She also gives examples of arguments found in the commentaries to show that compulsion was *allowed* in certain circumstances:

> Compulsion is permitted only in respect of those who have no religion, such as pagans ... Compulsion of pagans is ... not really compulsion. In fact some commentators claim that with the

pagans no compulsion occurred since they had no religion which they were compelled to abandon.

For the same reason, the conversion to Islam of children taken as captives in war is not considered compulsion. Since they have no religion of their own, children must adopt the religion of their captors.

Forced conversion to Islam ceases to be 'compulsion' if the convert later becomes convinced of the merits of Islam and embraces Islam sincerely out of conviction. Conversion following a war is not considered a compulsion since the conduct of war is guided by laws and rules which differ from those of peace time.

There is a tradition that Allah likes those who are dragged into Paradise in chains. This means that forced conversion ceases to be a 'compulsion', if and when the ultimate goal of attaining Paradise is achieved.[90]

She concludes:

This regress from tolerance to intolerance can be explained on at least two levels: (1) on the personal level, the Prophet had come to realize over the years, how utopian and unrealistic had been his expectations that Jews and others would join the growing Islamic community if approached gently and shown the essential similarity between Islam and their own faith; (2) on the national level, the Muslims themselves came to realize over the years that they could survive as a community without the approval of other religious communities. What is more, they were strong enough to fight these other communities and to prosper at their expense.[91]

The very fact that the commentators over a number of centuries wrestled with these verses in the way they did suggests that there were elements of coercion in their own history which they felt they had to explain.

Conclusion

If we ask whether Islam lived up to its basic principle of 'no compulsion in religion', our conclusion must be that while there have been examples of forcible conversion in different places and at different times, what is more important than such individual cases is the creation of the Islamic context in which individuals and groups were persuaded to adopt Islam. 'The purpose of conquest,' says William Shephard, a Christian scholar, 'was not to impose Islam but to create a situation in which Islam could have a hearing.'[92] Perhaps it would be more accurate to say that one of the purposes of conquest *was* to impose Islam, but by creating a total Islamic environment rather than by forcing individuals to become Muslims.

Levtzion similarly draws attention to the role of political power in the adoption of Islam throughout the Islamic Empire: 'Conversion was greatly advanced by the political and military predominance of the Muslims. In all cases of conversion from Christianity, Muslims had a political superiority, achieved by military conquest.'[93] Muslim historians like Dr Ikram and Professor Qureshi from Pakistan come to the same conclusion and stress 'the role of temporal power in creating a total Islamic environment as a precondition of the fostering of the right attitude and state of mind in individuals'.[94] In making the same point about the importance of political power, Fazlur Rahman is aware of the ambiguities and sensitivities which both Muslims and Christians must feel on this subject:

> Islam did have a political and economic hegemony but it did not have any missionary activity in any formal sense . . . It remains however true that because the Muslims had power many people were attracted towards Islam in order to be able to participate in that power structure. Whether this phenomenon can be characterized as ethically fair is a question which I do not think is open to discussion because there was never an active utilization of political power on the part of Muslims to attract non-Muslims. This does not mean to say that here and there there may not have been any cases of questionable methods of conversion, but this does not invalidate my position as a whole. In fact Christians are still being widely rumored to misuse the influential position of Western states to convert non-Christians to Christianity.[95]

In Chapters 6 and 7 we will be asking whether Christians in Britain can rightly be accused of misusing their influential position in education and in church–state relationships. In the meantime we may find in Chapter 3 that in Europe in recent years there has been more conversion from Christianity to Islam than from Islam to Christianity, and that certain aspects of the faith and practice of Islam in the past have just as strong appeal today. What is abundantly clear, however, is that in the West Islam does not have 'political superiority, achieved by military conquest'.

Notes

1. Nehemia Levtzion (ed.), *Towards a Comparative Study of Islamization*, Holmes and Meier, New York and London, 1979, pp. 12–13.
2. Mahmoud Ayoub, 'Religious Freedom and the Law of Apostasy in Islam', *Islamochristiana*, vol. 20, 1994, p. 77.
3. Many classical commentators interpreted the verse about the payment of *jizya* by *dhimmis* (9:29) and the verse about slaying the idolaters (9:5, known as the 'sword verse') as abrogating 2:256 and other such earlier verses.
4. A. Guillaume, *The Life of Muhammad: A translation of Ibn Ishaq's Sirat Rasul Allah*, Oxford University Press, 1955, pp. 561ff.
5. William Montgomery Watt, *Islamic Political Thought: The Basic Concepts*, Edinburgh University Press, 1968, p. 115.
6. Ibid., op. cit., p. 16.
7. Ibid., pp. 16–17.
8. Guillaume, op. cit., pp. 652ff.; and T.W. Arnold, *The Preaching of Islam: A history of the propagation of the Muslim faith*, Sheikh Muhammad Asraf, reprinted 1979 (first edition), Lahore, 1896, pp. 172–3.
9. Philip Hitti, *Islam and the West*, Van Nostrand, Princeton, 1962, p. 27.
10. Montgomery Watt, op. cit., pp. 18–19; cf Arnold, op. cit., p. 46.
11. Montgomery Watt, op. cit., p. 51.
12. Richard W. Bulliet, *Conversion to Islam in the Mediaeval Period: an essay in quantitative history*, Harvard University Press, pp. 1–2.
13. Levtzion, op. cit., p. 10.
14. Ibid., p. 18.
15. Ibid., p. 6.

16 Bulliet, op. cit., p. 131.
17 Levtzion, op. cit., pp. 12–13.
18 Bulliet, op. cit., p. 33.
19 Levtzion, op. cit., p. 66.
20 Ibid., p. 9.
21 Bulliet, op. cit., p. 34.
22 Levtzion, op. cit., p. 20.
23 Ibid., p. 19.
24 Bulliet, op. cit., pp. 35–7.
25 Ibid., p. 2.
26 Levtzion, op. cit., p. 9.
27 Larry Poston, *Islamic Da'wah in the West: Muslim missionary activity and the dynamics of conversion to Islam*, Oxford University Press, 1992, p. 15.
28 Ibid., p. 52.
29 Levtzion, op. cit., p. 32.
30 Bulliet, op. cit., p. 138.
31 Ibid., p. 138.
32 Levtzion, op. cit., p. 21.
33 Ibid., p. 20.
34 Ibid., p. 90.
35 Ibid., p. 237.
36 Arnold, op. cit., p. 5.
37 M. Shaban in Levtzion, op. cit., p. 24.
38 Levtzion op. cit., p. 15.
39 Arnold, op. cit., p. 356.
40 Levtzion, op. cit., pp. 16–17.
41 Arnold, op. cit., p. 129.
42 Fazlur Rahman, 'Non-Muslim Minorities in an Islamic State', *Journal of the Institute of Muslim Minority Affairs*, vol. 7, 1986, pp. 22–3.
43 Levtzion, op. cit., p. 21.
44 Ibid., p. 89.
45 Ibid., p. 11.
46 Arnold, op. cit., p. 46.
47 Ibid., pp. 103ff.
48 Ibid., p. 134.
49 Bulliet, op. cit., p. 41.
50 Ibid., p. 42.

51 Levtzion, op. cit., p. 9.
52 Ibid.
53 Ibid., p. 10.
54 Ibid., p. 9.
55 Arnold, op. cit., p. 294; P. Hardy in Levtzion, op. cit., pp. 13 and 81–2.
56 Levtzion, op. cit., p. 12.
57 Levtzion, op. cit., p. 11 and Jan Knappert in chapter 9, pp. 177–88.
58 Levtzion, op. cit., p. 154.
59 Ibid., pp. 85–6.
60 Arnold, op. cit., p. 271.
61 Levtzion, op. cit., p. 210.
62 Arnold, op. cit., pp. 56–7.
63 Ibid., p. 136.
64 Ibid., p. 96.
65 Ibid., pp. 196–7.
66 Levtzion, op. cit., p. 91.
67 Bulliet, op. cit., pp. 35–6.
68 Arnold, op. cit., pp. 200–2.
69 V.L. Menage in Levtzion, op. cit., p. 66.
70 Levtzion, op. cit., p. 208.
71 Ibid., p. 126.
72 Ibid., pp. 126–7.
73 Ibid., p. 360.
74 Arnold, op. cit., p. 106.
75 Levtzion, op. cit., p. 183.
76 Ibid., p. 21.
77 Arnold, op. cit., p. 74.
78 Ibid., pp. 172–3.
79 Ibid., pp. 118–19.
80 Ibid., p. 119.
81 Ibid., p. 142.
82 Mohammed Talbi, 'Religious Liberty: A Muslim perspective', *Islamochristiana*, vol. 11, 1985, p. 107.
83 Arnold, op. cit., pp. 47ff.
84 Levtzion, op. cit., p. 65.
85 Ibid., p. 64.
86 Arnold, op. cit., p. 261.
87 Levtzion op. cit., p. 78.

[88] Ibid., p. 11.
[89] Vardit Rispler-Chaim, 'There's No Compulsion in Religion (Qur'an 2:256): Freedom and religious belief in the Qur'an', *Bulletin*, Henry Martyn Institute, Hyderabad, July–Dec 1992, pp. 21–2.
[90] Ibid., pp. 22–3.
[91] Ibid., p. 28.
[92] William Shephard, 'The Right to be Wrong', *Journal of the Institute of Muslim Minority Affairs*, vol. 13:1, Jan 1992, p. 230.
[93] Levtzion, op. cit., p. 1.
[94] Peter Hardy in Levtzion, op. cit., p. 98.
[95] Fazlur Rahman, op. cit., pp. 22–3.

Three

Islamic Mission Today:
Is the West Ripe for Conversion?

Introduction

> Islam is . . . a missionary religion from its very inception. The
> Muslims are . . . missionaries of a world message and representa-
> tives of the greatest movement yet known to history (Muhammad
> Imran).[1]

> By bringing you here . . . Allah . . . has carved out a vocation for
> you, a new mission, and this mission is to save the West (Isma'il
> al-Faruqi).[2]

If the majority of Muslims in the West have come in search of
work or education, greater wealth or freedom, some at least
are able to recognize the hand of God at work in history and
believe that their presence in the West has some significance
in the plan of God. While they struggle to resist the pressures
of the ungodly society around them, some are confident
enough about their faith to commend it to the West as an
alternative to a declining Christianity, and to materialism,
hedonism, capitalism and socialism. In this chapter we try to
understand some Muslim thinking about its mission in the
West today. We then examine the statistics and the stories of
some who have converted to Islam, and attempt to assess the
chances of people in the West converting to Islam in larger
numbers.

1. The call to Islamic mission today

Most Muslims would recognize that the Qur'an sounds a clear call to all Muslims to engage in mission, and point to verses like this which encourage them to commend the faith of Islam to others: 'Invite (all) to the Way of thy Lord with wisdom and beautiful preaching; and argue with them in ways that are best and most gracious . . .' (Q. 16:125 Yusuf Ali's translation). Some have no hesitation is saying openly that mission is still of the essence of Islam, and that it is part of what is involved in being a Muslim in Western society today.

Khurram Murad, for example, a highly respected Muslim teacher and writer from Pakistan who lived for many years in the West and died in 1996, ended an address to the Annual Convention of the Islamic Society of North America in 1987 with a challenge to his audience to live and proclaim their Islamic faith in a secular environment. He expressed the belief that if they did so, America would eventually become a Muslim continent.[3] While Murad emphasized the value of a personal approach to individuals, he stated clearly what he believed to be the ultimate objective of Muslims in the West: the Islamic movement in the West 'should reaffirm and re-emphasize the concept of total change and supremacy of Islam in the Western society as its ultimate objective and allocate to it the highest priority'.[4] Similarly in an address to the Young Muslims in Britain in 1995 he said:

> It is no accident of history that you and the millions of Muslims reside here in the West, from Istanbul to Los Angeles. For no such accidents take place in a history directed by the All-Wise and All-Knowing God. You may have come for money, education, or a better material life, but He has placed you here for a purpose; to be ambassadors of the Prophet Muhammad to the West, the present day world leader. You are, therefore, on trial, and the choice is yours; whether to fail or succeed . . . The day will come when Britain will give up all 'isms' and established religions, and submit to the will of the Creator. That day Britain will become Islamic. Let that be your goal.[5]

Other Muslim speakers and writers have expressed the same objectives:

> The truth of Islam is not, or not chiefly, a theoretical truth, but also and prevalently law and customs felt as given by God, and obviously cannot be spread through personal conversion but only through physical conquest of the region to be converted (Bausani).[6]

> Our job is to make this country Muslim. Our religion orders us to go out and give people good news (Abd Al-Qadir).[7]

> Living in surrender to Allah cannot be actualized fully unless other people join us in our endeavour, unless the whole society lives in surrender. Hence, at least inviting others to join our venture, that is *Da'wah*, is an essential part of being a Muslim (Abul Hasan Ali Nadwi).[8]

Not all Muslims in Europe, however, share the same vision. Many are concerned primarily to keep their families and communities together, and see their religion as a private affair. Whenever there is any discussion about mission, they are often at pains to point out that a great deal of Islamic *da'wa* is directed to Muslims. They cannot feel complacent about a situation in which many Muslims have little contact with the mosque and are careless in the practice of their religion, and want to challenge them to a more consistent Islamic lifestyle. While there are a number of groups actively engaged in mission outside the Muslim community, many other Muslims know little or nothing about the activities of these groups, and would sometimes even dissociate themselves from them. If some Christians are more mission-minded than others, it is highly likely that there will be the same wide spectrum of views about mission in the Muslim community as there is among Christians.

In attempting therefore to assess how Muslims think about their 'mission' in the West, there are two particular dangers to be avoided. The first is the feeling that since *some* Muslims want to 'convert the West', *all* Muslims must want the same thing. The opposite danger is for people in the West to listen only to the more liberal voices in the Muslim community, and to discount completely the missionary intentions of a proportion of the Muslim community all over the world.

2. Statistics

Tomas Gerholm, in a 1983 study, wrote that 'no one knows how many converts there are in Western Europe'. He estimated that in France alone, however, there could be between fifty thousand and two hundred thousand converts.[9] The chapter on Conversion to Islam in Larry Poston's book, *Islamic Daʿwah in the West* (1992) is based on 72 testimonies of converts in the USA and Europe, gleaned from books, periodicals, pamphlets, and from answers to a questionnaire.[10] The following are the most significant statistics in Poston's survey:

(a) 69 per cent were men, and 31 per cent were women.
(b) 52 per cent came from a Christian background (including 10 Roman Catholics, 8 Protestants and 23 with no denomination given).
(c) The average age at the time of conversion was 31.4 years (for the Americans 29, for the Europeans 33.7).
(d) The average period between the rejection of the previous faith and the profession of Islam was 14.6 years; during this period they either had no faith or were exploring other options.

The best known converts among these 72 were: Cat Stevens (Yusuf Islam, well known as a British pop singer); Margaret Marcus (Maryam Jameelah, an American–Jewish academic); Muhammad Webb; Leopold Weiss (Muhammad Asad, born 1900, a Polish–Jewish journalist); Ivan Agneli (Abdul Hadi, died 1917, a Swedish painter); Roger Garaudy (Raja Garudi, born 1913, a French philosopher and politician); and Marmaduke Pickthall (author of the well-known English translation of the Qur'an).

The most recent comprehensive study of conversion in Britain, *Conversion to Islam: A Study of Native British Converts*, is the work of a Turkish scholar, Ali Köse.[11] It is based on interviews with 70 converts during 1990–1. The following are the main statistics concerning these converts:

(a) 71 per cent (50) were men and 29 per cent (20) were women.
(b) 60 per cent had at least a BA, while 20 per cent had advanced degrees.
(c) 94 per cent came from Christian backgrounds (73 per cent Church of England, 4 per cent Methodist and 17 per cent Roman Catholic), although the majority of these were not active church members; 6 per cent were Jews.
(d) 29 per cent had been involved in new religious movements.[12]
(e) Their ages were between 17 and 66.
(f) The average age at the time of conversion was 29.7 (with 61 per cent aged between 23 and 45).
(g) The total number of British converts at the present time is estimated to be between three and five thousand.[13]

Some of the best-known names among these converts are: Martin Lings, Gai Eaton, Ahmad Thomson, Abdul Hakim Winter, Meryl Wyn Davis, Sarah Malik, Ruqayah Khalil and Harfiyah Ball.

3. Significant factors in the experience of converts

In the studies by Gerholm, Poston and Köse, there are at least 11 factors that, in various combinations, have been important in the process of conversion.

(i) Dissatisfaction with a previous religion or ideology

Many converts are disillusioned with other faiths, such as Christianity, Judaism, humanism or Marxism. Several converts speak of Christian beliefs like the trinity, the deity of Christ, the atonement, transubstantiation and the special role of the clergy as being hard to accept. Muhammad Asad, a Jew, found the God of the Old Testament 'unduly concerned with ... ritual' and 'strangely preoccupied with the destinies of one particular nation, the Hebrews'.[14] Köse quotes a convert who describes how he gradually rejected the beliefs and practice of Christianity:

> From my mother I did have religious upbringing up to the age of 13. I had to take an active part in the church, but when I was 13 stopped going to church because I thought it was dead boring. Going to church and singing hymns just didn't appeal to me; I'd rather be out with my mates. I believed there was a God, but I didn't believe the other stuff. This thing with Jesus, God being Jesus and God, and the Holy Spirit, I couldn't accept it. They wouldn't answer my questions. Whenever I went to ask my mother a question she said, 'Ask the vicar.' If I asked the vicar, he wouldn't answer the question. We used to go round and round, and this circle never actually has come up with a solution. There were other things as well. I said to my mum once: 'If the New and the Old Testament are from the same God, how come in the Old Testament He is brutal and in the New He is kind?' It was a total change in personality. Eventually, I rejected everything when I was 15 and I didn't want anything to do with Christianity at all.[15]

(ii) Disillusionment with Western society

In the case of some converts it seems that Christianity is blamed for the degeneration of Western society. 'Considerable disgust is often expressed,' says Gerholm, 'at the low moral standards of Western countries, which are believed to reflect on the weakness of Christianity. Many speak of their disillusionment with much of Western civilization, and in particular with its "one-sided materialism".'[16] In other cases, however, their disillusionment with the West has little to do with Christianity. Köse speaks of one convert, Adam, who 'had begun to hate the Western way of life for being so entrenched in capitalism'[17] and comments that 'his conversion was brought on as a result of his distate of capitalism and thereby the Western way of life rather than his theological disillusionment with Christianity'.[18] He speaks of others in the 1960s who 'were driven into Islam by the uneasiness they felt in their culture, not because Islam was "true" or the "best" religion. "It was actually a sort of Islamised version of the new left politics and philosophy. It had much more to do with students' revolution in Paris and stuff like that", said an early participant.'[19] This was particularly true of converts who joined certain Sufi groups, since, according to Köse, they were 'rejecting Western culture rather than traditional religion'.[20] In another case rebellion against Western society was motivated by more personal reasons:

> I think throughout everything with me there is an element of rebellion. I've always rebelled against something. If it wasn't my father, it would have to be something else when he died. So I rebelled against the society . . . the next rebellion perhaps was initially the thought of joining a religion (Islam) which was obviously so hated by the people in the West.[21]

Disillusionment with society creates a new hunger for spiritual reality, with the result that:

> The individual takes spirituality as the new answer and develops the belief that the spiritual realm holds the key to the resolution of his problems and the society's social problems. So it is observable that the shift is not only about one's departure from Christianity to Islam, but it is also about one's withdrawal from secular to sacred . . .[22]

> The over-secularisation of society led them to seek for an alternative way of life. They initially became interested in Islam because they felt that it had strong, clear values on things they felt concerned about. Their revolt was not directed against religious beliefs, but against certain practices (like moral permissiveness) legitimised by their former religion . . . It is apparent that this shift is not about departure from (nominal) Christianity to Islam, but it is about a growing tendency towards the sacred or spiritual.[23]

(iii) Conversion through marriage

While a non-Muslim woman who marries a Muslim man is not obliged to accept Islam, a considerable number of women have in practice accepted Islam at the time of marriage or soon after. In Köse's survey, five people (four men and one woman) converted before marriage in order to be able to marry a Muslim spouse; 20 per cent were married or engaged to a Muslim partner when they converted.

(iv) Personal contact with Muslims

Many mention the influence of individual Muslims they have met, in many cases while travelling overseas. Among the first British converts to Islam at the end of the nineteenth century and the first part of the twentieth century, according to Köse, 'the most overriding character . . . is that many of them had worked in Muslim lands, especially in India, and had been impressed by the faith and conduct of Muslim colleagues. Also there was a large number of transient visitors to Britain, often students from the Muslim world.'[24] In this century, many of the European men were serving in the army during the two world wars.[25] Muhammad Asad describes a discussion with a provincial governor in Afghanistan who said to him, 'But you are a Muslim . . . only you do not know it yourself.'[26] In Köse's survey, 23 per cent were first introduced to Islam while travelling to Muslim countries.[27] One convert, Jason, describes his experience in Egypt:

> I did a lot of travelling around Egypt and just talked to the people. What surprised me was the extent to which so many people adhere to religion. It struck me because over here although we are all Christians we don't really adhere to Christian teachings. In Egypt you get into a car and the taxi driver has a copy of the Koran. This was very shocking for someone like myself who lives in a country where people are not that dedicated towards a particular religion.[28]

Isma'il al-Faruqi believed that the family is the 'best tool' for Islamic *da'wa* because of the way it can present the values of Islam in the West. He used to urge Muslims to make it a rule to invite non-Muslims to visit their family once a week.[29] And according to Köse, 'Most Muslims believe that living a Muslim life style is sufficient to attract others to the religion.'[30]

(v) The Qur'an

Reading the Qur'an has played an important part in the experience of many converts. Cat Stevens' brother, for example, gave him a copy of the Qur'an which he had bought during a visit to Jerusalem.[31] Köse quotes several who describe the powerful effect of the Qur'an on them:

> The more I read, the more I felt that I was a Muslim and I took the *shahada* when I was 30.[32]

> It [the Qur'an] was saying 'Don't do this, don't do that!' And I was thinking, 'Well, whoever has written this has been watching me for the last few years. It was written all down what I have been doing wrong. It was really a shock'.[33]

> I became Muslim in the absence of a Muslim, just through the study of the Koran.[34]

> It was the Koran that really made me Muslim.[35]

(vi) A complete philosophy of life

Many converts speak of finding answers to intellectual questions about the meaning of life. Islam has explained for them humankind's place in the universe and proclaimed 'the responsibility of man, a future life, and a day of judgement. It had answers to their questions like "what is man's place in the universe?" '[36] For some converts it is the integration of the intellectual and the practical, the spiritual and the material, the individual and the social, which proves to be so compelling. So for Maryam Jameelah, 'Islam provided its adherents with a complete, comprehensive way of life in which the relation of the individual to society and the material to the spiritual were balanced in perfect harmony.' Similarly another convert, Wieslaw Zejierski, believed 'that mankind could be guided only by a religion which presented a perfect and complete code of individual and social life'.[37] A similar sentiment is expressed by Garaudy who speaks frequently about the equilibrium, harmony and unity of Islam. Thus, according to Gerholm, 'Garaudy's image of Islam as a model for a possible synthesis of previous civilizations is very much in accordance with the Islamic image of itself as a synthesis and correction of the previously revealed religions.'[38] One of the converts in Köse's study sums up how they understand the comprehensiveness of Islam in the British context:

> Islam affects society and it is a stabilising force. This was a very important factor in my conversion. I think one of the weaknesses of Christianity is that it is prepared to change its rules to suit changes in society and, therefore, it is no longer a stabilising factor. It follows the secular need. The society is secular and the Christians can't keep up. That's why they are changing . . . I've always felt that religion should be a stabilising factor. I think man needs to have rule and order. We are not animals.[39]

(vii) Simplicity and rationality

Twenty per cent of Poston's converts speak of the 'simplicity' of Islam as an important factor in their conversion, and 75 per cent say they were attracted by some aspect of the teaching of Islam. For one, Islam is 'simple and straightforward, free from elaborations which cannot be believed'.[40] Islam is perceived to be utterly rational: 'Islam is the only system known to man which is strictly in harmony with reason and science.' 'Islam appeals to one's reason.'[41] A British convert explains how he has responded to this aspect of Islam:

> Everything made sense and was reasonable, everything added up, but there were one or two aspects of Islam which I couldn't quite understand at first. They were not fundamentally contradictory problems, they were problems which might have been correct or might have been wrong and so I took the attitude on these issues to accept them and believe them perhaps in the future . . . Of course, I can understand these much better now.[42]

Closely related to the perception of Islam being simple and rational is the feeling that Islam is a 'natural religion', 'the religion of nature'. Islam is seen as 'simply a programme of life in accord with the "laws of nature" which God has decreed upon His creation; and its supreme achievement is a complete coordination of the spiritual and the material aspects of human existence'.[43] For these reasons, the majority of converts interviewed in a research project on conversions in the 1980s questioned the use of the word 'conversion' to describe the profession of Islam. They preferred to see the transition as 'a continuity, a growth, a fulfilment'.[44]

(viii)   Moral and ethical standards

While few turn to Islam out of a sense of guilt over sins committed in the past, there is often a sense that whatever wrong has been done in the past has been wiped out. 'The converts felt,' according to Köse, 'that they were cleansed from all the dregs of the past. They felt that by accepting Islam they were wiped clean of their former sins and the "bad deeds" they had committed. It is, in fact, the Islamic precept that made them feel that way. According to Islam once one is converted, he is cleansed of his previous sins.'[45] Establishing a relationship with God creates a sense of stability and moral purpose: 'To me Islam is like finding God again. With Islam I am back in contact directly with God, whereas over the last 20 years I haven't really. It is also reconfirming or strengthening my moral and ethical outlook on life.'[46]

For many, however, it is the clear moral framework which attracts them rather than any offer of forgiveness for the past. Some have been attracted by what they see as a faith which sets realistic moral standards in contrast to the unreasonably high and other-worldly standards of Christianity on the one hand and the low moral standards generally accepted in the West on the other. One British man admitted that he worshipped 'nobility and courage' and was impressed by the virility and masculinity of Muslim males.[47] Several mention in particular Islamic teaching and practice in the area of sex and marriage:

> They didn't drink, they didn't have any relationships outside marriage and they were very happy not doing it and they were very confident in arguing these points . . . I read the Koran one month before I became a Muslim and the verses about morality and relationships, and there were so many verses about what is

right, what is wrong. This is the most fundamental part that gives you a framework. Christianity says, 'You must choose right as opposed to wrong', but it gives you no framework. Islam gives you the basis. It gives you personal hygiene, five times prayer a day, etc. There is no way you can avoid Islam during your day. You have to think about God, you have to think about your work-mates, your family, etc.[48]

My initial contact with Islam came through Muslim friends at the university. I didn't ask them any questions about Islam and they rarely mentioned it. It only came up in general conversation. But the family structure attracted me. The women want to be woman, not man, and the men go off to work and the women remain woman in the home. Very nice. Yes, I like this. They don't try to get drunk all night. They have moral values; they don't have sex before marriage with as many people as possible. This is the kind of woman I want to marry. I could see this directly from the way they live their life-styles. You can see the women are not running off with anyone.[49]

(ix) Disgust with racism

Many are impressed with the universal brother- and sister-hood of Islam, in which they believe there is no place for racial discrimination. Both in the USA and in Britain, for example, many blacks feel that Christianity is the white person's religion, and have become Muslims in reaction to the racism they have experienced. Zaki Badawi has pointed out that Salman Rushdie's *The Satanic Verses* was as much about racism as about Islam: 'Rushdie clearly feels strongly the cold blast of racialism – indeed more of his *Satanic Verses* is about that than an attack on Islam itself.' In the same article he went on to express his hopes for the author in these terms: 'I believe Rushdie will probably return to Islam. He has nowhere else to turn but back to his roots – and British racism may be thanked for that.'[50] Malcolm X initially joined the Black Muslim group known as 'The Nation of Islam', but later left it to become an orthodox Muslim. Some words that he wrote while on pilgrimage to Mecca explain why the apparent absence of racism in Islam was such an important factor in his decision:

Never have I witnessed such sincere hospitality and overwhelming spirit of true brotherhood as is practised by people of all colours and races here in this Holy Land, the home of Abraham, Muhammad, and all the other prophets of the Holy Scriptures. For the past week, I have been utterly speechless and spell-bound by the graciousness I see displayed all around me by people *of all colours* . . . America needs to understand Islam, because this is the one religion that erases from its society the race problem . . . During the past eleven days here in the Muslim world, I have eaten from the same plate, drunk from the same glass, and slept in the same bed (or in the same rug) – while praying to the same God – with fellow Muslims, whose eyes were the bluest of the blue, whose hair was the blondest of the blond, and whose skin was the whitest of the white.[51]

(x) Special appeal to women

Several women in the two surveys have been impressed by the respect shown to women by Islam, explaining, for example, that the wearing of the veil makes it harder for them to be treated as sex objects. Maryam Jameelah found the 'strictness' of Islam a haven in comparison with the immorality of society in New York.[52] Some seem to have reacted against the feminist movement in the West.[53] This was the comment of one convert:

It was the Koran that really made me Muslim. The verses related to woman, the way it speaks of woman as having the same right as man in marriage struck me. It says: 'man and woman were created equal with different roles'. It is not necessary for a woman to put up with a bad marriage. Because Islam says that 'both of you should be equally happy'. Both have equal responsibility and he should treat you with respect.[54]

(xi) Sufism

Poston believes that in the USA 'Sufism . . . apparently has not played a major role in establishing a direct Muslim witness.'[55] Köse, however, believes that Britain is no exception to the rule that Sufism has been one of the major factors in conversion to

Islam throughout history.[56] No fewer than 33 per cent of the converts he interviewed had either come to Islam through Sufism or were currently involved in Sufism, and 14 per cent (nine men and one woman) had had mystical experiences before embracing Islam. He therefore speaks of Sufism as 'the major force behind conversion to Islam in Britain'.[57] Three well-known British converts, James Dickie, Gai Eaton and Martin Lings, and two Swiss, Frithjof Shuon and Titus Burckhardt, were attracted by Sufism.

There are five factors in particular which may help to account for the attraction of Sufi expressions of Islam in the Western context:

(a) It appeals to people of many kinds who are engaged in a spiritual quest. They have been seeking 'to master spiritual and/or physical disciplines in order to achieve a state of enlightenment and self-harmony'.[58] The spiritual guide within the Sufi tradition, the sheikh, the *pir* or *murshid*, is able to help others on their spiritual journey.

(b) Sufism offers access to a source of spiritual power. Thus one convert says: 'I believe that a shaykh is able to transmit something, the *barakah* [blessing or power] . . .'[59]

(c) It offers both intellectual answers and spiritual insight about the meaning of life. One convert outlines the 'answer' that he has found in Islam: 'Islam has given me absolute hope, hope of Reality. I know what "Reality" is. I know the answers that all the mystics are always talking about. What greater mystery is there to know than Allah? I know the answer to the question "what is the meaning of life?", we had come from Allah and we are going back to Allah. So what more do I need to know? We are created beings. That's what our purpose is. Otherwise if we didn't believe that, there would be no purpose, we would be just an extraordinary accident like a lot of people think. I know we are not that.'[60]

(d) Sufism has often been associated with left-wing politics.[61]

(e) Sufis seem to have little taste for the kind of doctrinal controversy and polemics in which Muslims have often engaged in the past, especially with Christians. Rather than seeing Jesus as the 'Son of God', they see him as a model of the kind of relationship with God which any believer can enjoy, and think of him as their 'exemplary *par excellence*'.[62] When asked about important differences between Muslims and Christians in their beliefs about Jesus, the Sufi Sheikh Nazim gave the answer: 'Keep your belief. They are Christians and keep their beliefs. No need for discussion. Don't touch the beliefs of people . . . The important thing is that if your beliefs are taking you to the Lord, it is all right . . . It is a point that 1400 years of discussion has never solved. Therefore we do not disturb people through their beliefs . . .'[63]

(xii)   Community and individualism

While Islam stresses that every individual must stand before God on his/her own, it also holds out the possibility of belonging to a local and world-wide community. Thus Poston believes that in the Western context, Islam's emphasis on the communal is balanced by the feeling that 'in Islam contact with God depends on man himself'. This means that 'the believer does not need any mediation; Islam does not need priesthood'. He concludes: 'This aspect of Muslim theology appealed strongly to the individualism of western men.'[64] One British convert describes how he has experienced the communal aspect of Islam: 'When you do your prayer in the mosque you have physical contact with another human; you touch the man standing next to you. When you meet somebody you shake hands. In British society you don't have any contact apart from girlfriends and things. I think it is a human bond that they miss. Religion in this society doesn't have any place, it is something you do on Sunday.'[65]

(xiii)   Supernatural phenomena

Out of the 72 testimonies examined by Poston, only three speak of 'supernatural experiences' of any kind. In one of these the Prophet Muhammad appeared in a dream. Another person describes a dream in which he saw smoke rising from the earth, and the word 'Islam' being formed out of the light which came

from the smoke. The third spoke of awaking one morning to
see a 'dazzling bright light like a great star', out of which came
'the beautiful voice of a young man'. Although the voice
quoted verses from the Gospel of John, this person understood
that Jesus was encouraging her to convert to Islam.[66]

Poston suggests that 'since Muslims do not emphasize supernatural phenomena in connection with conversion . . .
historians of Islam considered the experience of conversion to
be normative and therefore not necessary to report.'[67] Early
Islamic sources reported many conversions to Islam during the
life of the Prophet, like that of Hamza, the Prophet's uncle, who
at first opposed Muhammad, but later changed his mind when
he saw Muslims suffering for their faith. Similarly Umar, who
later became the second caliph, was so angry at his sister's
conversion to Islam that he set out to kill Muhammad. When
he struck his sister, he was filled with remorse, and on hearing
the passage from the Qur'an which she had been reading,
exclaimed 'How beautiful, how sublime it is! . . . Lead me to
Muhammad that I may tell him of my conversion.' Muslims
would say that these changes of mind came about in an entirely
natural way, without any obvious supernatural intervention.
This is why, according to Poston, acceptance of Islam for many
'did not involve an upheaval . . . On the contrary, it appears
that it is possible for one to step effortlessly into the religion.'[68]

Köse tells the story of George who, while with the British
army in Yemen, had wandered into a building in a graveyard,
and instinctively took off his shoes, noticing the beautiful smell
in the room. It was only later that he found out that the building
he had been in was the tomb of a saint, and as a result of this
experience, came to believe that it was the saint's blessing
which made him a Muslim.[69] The importance of supernatural
phenomena in some kinds of Sufism is recognized by Köse
who sees the ability to perform some miraculous acts (*karamat*)
as 'one of the most common indicators of being a shaikh'.[70]

(xiv) Emotional experiences

While several converts have spoken of 'a feeling of peace
and happiness', there is a remarkable absence of emotional

experiences associated with conversion. The conclusion drawn by Poston is that 'conversions to Islam . . . differ significantly from conversions to Christianity in that they appear to be "conversions of the head" (i.e. intellectual) rather than "conversions of the heart" (i.e. emotional).'[71] Remorse for sin and fear of judgment do *not* seem to have been important factors. Only one person said that her conversion was in part due to 'many sins and mistakes'. On the contrary many believe that the idea of original sin is repulsive and have said that they were attracted to the more optimistic view of human nature found in Islam.[72] Köse makes the similar observation, noting that 'conversions did not occur as a direct result of the emotional turmoil of personal distress'.[73] For one convert, Charlie, for example, 'leaving Christianity was an emotional experience, but embracing Islam was an intellectual process'.[74] For another the test of truth is very pragmatic: 'I was looking for something that worked, something that gives you integration and strength. That was what I was looking for. Whatever it was I did not care what kind of mad beliefs. But if it worked as far as I was concerned that must be true because it works.'[75] Köse concludes that 'it is important to note that the potential convert seems to test out the new faith experimentally, rather than embracing it without thought. The decision is therefore characterised as being intellectual which is the end result of a deliberate choice made after careful examination and consideration rather than emotional.'[76]

If we compare this list of factors with those in Chapter 2, the most obvious factors which are evident in *both* situations are: Islam seen as liberation (for example from oppressive rule or from racism); the simplicity and rationality of Islamic belief; and the role of Sufism.

4. Challenges facing Islamic mission in the West

Muslim communities in Western countries are likely to increase in numbers partly through immigration and partly through a higher than average birth-rate. If Islam in the West is not only to survive, but also to grow both in numbers and

influence, it would seem that it faces serious challenges in the
following areas:

(i)   Nominalism and assimilation

If this has been a constant fear of Jewish communities in the West
it must now be a real fear for Muslims also. Those who have no
links with a mosque and make no effort to maintain an Islamic
lifestyle are regarded as in danger of being assimilated to
Western society.

(ii)   The impression of being a foreign religion

The majority of Muslim communities in Britain have come
originally from Pakistan, Bangladesh, India or the Middle East,
and often want to maintain strong links with their country of
origin. Many of their leaders and teachers at the local level
have been trained overseas and do not give the impression of
wanting to be part of British society.[77] Although some Muslim
groups, like the Abd al-Qadir as-Sufi movement, have made a
special attempt to attract Western converts, their numbers are
still comparatively small.[78] There are few white British Muslims in positions of leadership, and there are probably still not
enough Muslims from non-Muslim backgrounds to demon-
strate what a thoroughly contextualized form of British Islam
would look like.

Eighty-one per cent of the British converts in Köse's survey
have adopted Islamic names, although some use their new
name only within the Muslim community.[79] The change of name
suggests to outsiders a change of culture as well. The converts
themselves say that they do not cease to feel 'British' or 'English'.
They maintain elements of Christian religious traditions in their
lifestyle, like celebrating Christmas and exchanging presents
with family and friends. Many of them find ways of being both
British and Muslim:

> Most of the converts seem not to have changed culturally. They
> have not wiped out their culture completely, even though
> they have undergone some cultural changes over the years. They

do not feel that by becoming Muslim they have been 'Arabised' or 'Pakistanised'. They feel that they are still English/British and see no conflict between cultures before becoming Muslim and afterwards. They feel it is just as valid to be a British Muslim as being a Nigerian Muslim or an Egyptian Muslim.[80]

Köse gives examples of the way a man and a woman have worked through the question of being Muslim in a British cultural context:

Islam is a religion that overlays the culture. The religion which gave rise to the British culture is, of course, Christianity. And a particular style of Christianity is not actually incompatible with Islam. The thing which helped the culture evolve is in itself quite akin to Islam, therefore, Islam and European culture should be able to sit quite comfortably. Islam and Europe are so closely connected over the last thousand years. Simply by following British culture and adopting the religion of Islam there wouldn't be any conflict. I am proud of being an Englishman. Being a Pakistani or whatever wouldn't necessarily bring me any closer to Islam.[81]

If you are English and you are brought up in this country and then you become a Muslim, you have to try and find your own way of doing things because you continue to be English. The whole thing of a code of behaviour or a code of dress would be at the back of my mind whatever I was trying to do. So it is not enough simply to start wearing a veil because essentially what you are trying to do is change yourself inside. So I feel for myself I have to go, to some extent, by the accepted norms of the society I live in. So what is regarded as modest dress (long sleeves and a high neck and the skirt under knees), would be the sort of standards I would set for myself. I mean I don't wear a scarf when I am out. Because basically, I don't feel comfortable. That might change as time goes on, but I don't really want to draw attention to myself.[82]

(iii)   The image of Islam in other countries

Islam is still too closely associated in many people's minds with negative images in other countries. People who are aware of the violence of Algerian Islamists in France, the Islamization policy of the present Sudanese government, the Iranian government's refusal to lift the *fatwa* against Salman Rushdie and the policy of the Taliban that excludes women from public life in Afghanistan find it hard to make a total separation between these actions and the religion of Islam. Many Muslims will dissociate themselves from the policies of these governments, just as the majority of Protestants and Catholics dissociate themselves from the activities of Protestant and Catholic terrorist groups in Northern Ireland and see their activities as an expression of nationalist feeling rather than of Christian faith. But when policies and actions in these countries are justified in the name of Islam, the outside world inevitably finds it hard to distinguish between the actions of certain Islamic governments and the ideals of Islam.

(iv)   The strictness of Islam: an asset or a liability?

While this is an aspect of Islam that has undoubtedly attracted many individuals, it is hard to see how in the permissive society of the West, large numbers of people are likely to be attracted by a religion that requires quite a strict code of life. Muslims like to present Islam as a holistic religion that has something to say about *every* aspect of life and prescribes many details of personal life. A religion that makes so much of the concept of law may not commend itself too easily to generations who have been encouraged to think in terms of freedom, personal choice and self-fulfilment.

(v)   The representation of Muslims in the wider community

While Muslims make much of the fact that Islam is not divided into thousands of denominations in the way that the Christian church is, it has to be recognized that, as Philip Lewis has pointed out, 'Islam is less homogenous and less static than outsiders commonly suppose.'[83] Many mosques serve particular ethnic groups – Pakistani, Bangladeshi and so on. Some represent a more pietistic and personal approach to Islam, while others have a much more overtly political agenda on the local or national level. As far as one can see, however, there does not seem to be anything comparable in the Muslim community to the structures of religious denominations that are understood in the West, like the parish, the diocese or the synod. They make a great deal of the fact that they have no clergy, bishops, archbishops or pope. But how then do they organize themselves, and how do they expect to be represented in conversations with others? Islam does not seem to have anything comparable to the ecumenical movement and the World Council of Churches. As a result, while opinions are expressed by a variety of individuals, institutions and organizations, it is not always easy for people outside the Muslim community to understand how widely these opinions are held among the Muslim community.

(vi) Influence over the democratic processes

As long as Muslims remain a minority in Britain and the rest of Europe, it will be extremely difficult for them to exert enough pressure within the ordinary democratic processes to enable them to create the kind of Islamic environment that some of them would like to see. While this no doubt remains their ultimate goal, much of their activity in the public realm at present is directed at improving the condition of their communities and enabling them to create an environment for their immediate family and community that is more conducive to the practice of Islam.

(vii) How well can Islam engage with the modern world?

The response of many Muslims to Salman Rushdie's *The Satanic Verses* illustrates some of the problems they face in coming to terms with certain aspects of the modern world. It is not hard to appreciate the pain and anger experienced by Muslims all over the world when they heard reports about the content of the book – the irreverent poking of fun at the Prophet, the crude and blasphemous language, the fantasies in which, for example, the prostitutes in the brothel in 'Mecca' give themselves the names of the wives of the Prophet, and so on. Here was someone born and bred as a Muslim who had ceased to be a Muslim, and was now using his inside information about Islamic history and culture and employing a thoroughly Western artistic medium to pour scorn on traditions that are precious to all Muslims.

The challenge of the book, however, goes much deeper than this, since it questions the very idea of divine revelation. For if Muhammad on one occasion (as reported in reliable Islamic sources) recited a revelation which he believed had come from God, but later retracted it because he was told that it had in fact come from Satan – if this happened once, how do we know it couldn't have happened more often? How, for that matter, can we know that anything purporting to be divine revelation is in fact from God, and not the product of a person's own imagination?

The challenge that Rushdie is presenting to Islam at this point is the epistemological question that is probably the most fundamental philosophical challenge modernity addresses to any faith or ideology: how do you know that this is true? How indeed can you know that anything is true? To many observers it looks as if Muslims find this question very hard to address in any other way than by reasserting the conviction that the Qur'an is divine revelation and by saying that any questioning of this assumption amounts to unbelief. Thirty years ago Wilfred Cantwell-Smith wrote some words about the way he sensed that Muslims would sooner or later have to face up to these difficult questions:

> Muslims do not read the Qur'an and conclude that it is divine; rather, they believe that it is divine, and then they read it . . . The Muslim world . . . is moving into what may possibly become a profound crisis . . . in that it . . . is just beginning to ask this question, instead of being content only with answering it. Young people in Lahore and Cairo, labour leaders in Jakarta and Istanbul, are beginning to ask their religious thinkers, and beginning to ask themselves, 'Is the Qur'an the word of God?' Answering this question has been the business of the Muslim world for over thirteen centuries. Asking it is a different matter altogether, haunting and ominous.[84]

Has Islam – especially in the West – begun to find ways of coping with the acids of modern scepticism and doubt? Olivier

Roy in his book *The Failure of Political Islam* points to another area in which Islam (particularly in its more fundamentalist expressions) seems to have difficulty in coming to terms with modernity:

> The defensive rigidity of neofundamentalism ... demonstrates its inability to incorporate modernity ... The culture that threatens Muslim society is neither Jewish nor Christian; it is a world culture of consumption and communication, a culture that is secular, atheist, and ultimately empty; it has no values or strategies, but it is already here, in the cassette and the transistor, present in the most remote village. This culture can withstand any reappropriation and rereading. It is a code and not a civilization. Neofundamentalism is seeking its devil in a different god, but does not see the desert within.[85]

(viii) Can Islam provide viable economic and political answers?

While the Muslim communities in the West are hardly in a position to enter debates on politics or economics at the macro level, the rest of the world is no doubt watching to see what the governments in the world that make the loudest profession of Islam are able to do to solve political and economic problems in their own countries. Do the Mullahs in Iran, for example, know how to run a modern economy? Can the Muslim Brotherhood and other Islamist groups in Egypt provide the material means and the motivation to feed the poorest in their society? Does Islamic banking really provide a valid alternative to capitalism and socialism? When Olivier Roy asks 'can it (Islam) offer an economic alternative or deeply transform a society?' he believes that the answer seems to be no:

> The Islamization of the economy is ... largely rhetorical. The failure of the Iranian revolution to transform the society chips away at the dream of a purely Islamic economy. All a devout Muslim can do is bring his activities into conformity with the *sharia*; to do so, he can either withdraw from the modern world or utilize the instruments for the purification of profits, the

Islamic banks and windows [sic]. But as far as the economy goes, these institutions function between two models, neither of which is specifically Islamic: the declining model of the centralized, socialist-leaning state, or the triumphant model of liberalism and capitalism.[86]

The more Muslims suggest that Islam can solve all the problems of the West, the more the West may have to ask Muslims whether Islam has 'delivered the goods' in Islamic countries and carried out the dreams that it has held out to their people.

Conclusion

What signs can we see that Islam is likely to be able, in al-Faruqi's words, to 'save the West'? Can we foresee the day that Khurram Murad set as his goal when 'Britain will become Islamic'? On the basis of what we have seen in this chapter, the most obvious answer seems to be that while Islam may continue to attract a number of individual converts, it is not likely to see conversion in large numbers. Muslims in the West have not been able to create the Islamic institutions, or the Islamic ambience that they did during the first centuries in the middle East. Having little access to the corridors of power they will probably remain a minority – though perhaps a more vocal one – for many years to come. Köse, himself a Muslim, ends his study of 70 British converts with an admission that the attractive features of Islam may not be strong enough to counteract the difficulties facing the Muslim community and win significant numbers of new converts:

> Muslims living in Britain believe that the modesty of Muslim women, the stability of Muslim family life, the absence of drinks, drugs, and sex-related crimes and the overall discipline of Muslims living in the West will itself send powerful signals to non-Muslims, since the moral values of Christianity are diminishing in the society. However, these attractions of Islam may be offset by lack of effective missionary strategy and by the perception of Islam in the West as a religion of half-civilized Middle Eastern people.[87]

Notes

[1] Larry Poston, *Islamic Da'wah in the West: Muslim missionary activity and the dynamics of conversion to Islam*, Oxford University Press, 1992, p. 111.

[2] Isma'il al-Faruqi, 'The Path of Da'wah in the West', UK Islamic Mission, London, 1986, p. 25.

[3] Larry Poston, 'Da'wa in the West', in *The Muslims of America*, Yvonne Yazbeck Haddad (ed.), Oxford University Press, 1991, p. 130.

[4] Quoted in Poston, *Islamic Da'wah in the West*, op. cit., p. 82.

[5] Shaikh Khurram Murad, 'Message to Young Muslims', *Q-News International*, no. 248–50, 27 Dec 1996–9 Jan 1997, p. 43.

[6] Quoted in Poston, *Islamic Da'wah in the West*, op. cit., p. 52.

[7] Quoted in Ali Köse, *Conversion to Islam: A study of native British converts*, Kegan Paul, London and New York, 1996, p. 184.

[8] Quoted in Poston, 'Da'wa in the West', op. cit., p. 212.

[9] Tomas Gerholm and Yngve (sic) George Litham (eds.), *The New Islamic Presence in Europe*, Mansell, London, 1988, p. 264. Kate Zebiri, writing in 1997, suggested that 'there are probably 8,000 converts to Islam in Britain today.' 'Why do people convert to Islam', in *Partnership News*, Centre for Black and White Christian Partnership, No. 19, Winter 1997/98, p. 13.

[10] The methodology is explained in Poston, *Islamic Da'wah in the West*, op. cit., pp. 160ff.

[11] The methodology is explained in Köse, op. cit., pp. 2ff.

[12] Köse, op. cit., p. 190.

[13] Ibid., p. 19.

[14] Gerholm and Litham, op. cit., p. 268.

[15] Köse, op. cit., pp. 52–3.

[16] Gerholm, op. cit., p. 271.

[17] Köse, op. cit., p. 70.

[18] Ibid., p. 71.

[19] Ibid., p. 176.

[20] Ibid., p. 194.

[21] Ibid., p. 56.

[22] Ibid., p. 22.

[23] Ibid., p. 191.

[24] Ibid., p. 19.

25 Ibid., pp. 164 and 173.
26 Gerholm, op. cit., p. 169.
27 Köse, op. cit., p. 112.
28 Ibid., p. 103.
29 Ibid., p. 52.
30 Ibid., p. 26.
31 Poston, *Islamic Da'wah in the West*, op. cit., p. 173.
32 Köse, op. cit., p. 90.
33 Ibid., pp. 55–6.
34 Ibid., p. 101.
35 Ibid., p. 111.
36 Ibid., p. 192.
37 Poston, *Islamic Da'wah in the West*, op. cit., p. 178.
38 Gerholm, op. cit., p. 271.
39 Köse, op. cit., pp. 75–6.
40 Poston, *Islamic Da'wah in the West*, op. cit., p. 176.
41 Ibid., p. 177.
42 Köse, op. cit., p. 113.
43 Gerholm, op. cit., p. 270.
44 Ibid., p. 272.
45 Köse, op. cit., p. 129.
46 Ibid., p. 72.
47 Poston, *Islamic Da'wah in the West*, op. cit., pp. 163–4.
48 Köse, op. cit., p. 64.
49 Ibid., p. 101.
50 Zaki Badawi, quoted by Paul Martin in, 'Spurn the Book, Spare the Man', *Guardian Weekly*, 5 March 1989.
51 Köse, op. cit., p. 102.
52 Poston, op. cit., p. 175.
53 Ibid., p. 164.
54 Köse, op. cit., p. 54.
55 Poston, op. cit., p. 128.
56 Köse, op. cit., p. 142.
57 Ibid., p. 20.
58 Ibid., p. 155.
59 Ibid., p. 159.
60 Ibid., p. 151.
61 Gerholm, op. cit., p. 265.
62 Köse, op. cit., p. 144.

63 Ibid., p. 174.
64 Ibid., p. 178.
65 Ibid., p. 67.
66 Poston, op. cit., p. 170.
67 Ibid., p. 158.
68 Ibid., p. 169.
69 Köse, op. cit., pp. 105–6.
70 Ibid., p. 165.
71 Poston, op. cit., pp. 169–71.
72 Ibid., pp. 174–5.
73 Köse, op. cit., p. 192.
74 Ibid., p. 84.
75 Ibid., p. 170.
76 Ibid., p. 123.
77 See Philip Lewis, *Islamic Britain: Religion, Politics and Identity among British Muslims*, I.B. Tauris, 1994, chapter 5.
78 Köse, op. cit., pp. 175–80.
79 Ibid., p. 128.
80 Ibid., p. 135.
81 Ibid.
82 Ibid., p. 131.
83 Philip Lewis, 'Being Muslim and Being British' in *Desh Pardesh: The South Asian presence in Britain*, Roger Ballard (ed.), Hurst, London, 1994, p. 57.
84 Wilfred Cantwell-Smith, *Questions of Religious Truth*, Gollancz, London, 1967, pp. 48–9.
85 Olivier Roy, *The Failure of Political Islam*, I.B. Tauris, London, 1994, p. 203.
86 Ibid., pp. 131 and 145.
87 Köse, op. cit., p. 194.

Four

The War of Words:
Polemics, Apologetics or Dialogue?

Introduction

> It is not possible to teach the life of Christ except by destroying
> and condemning the law of Machomet Muhammad (Robert
> Holcot, fourteenth century).[1]

> There must needs be an apologetic literature, unafraid of contro-
> versial points. Silence, he felt, was tantamount to denial of the
> truth he knew and lived (Constance Padwick writing about
> Temple Gairdner of Cairo).[2]

> Islam has to be open at a deep level to what Christians are saying,
> just as Christians have to be open to what you [Muslims] are
> saying (Kenneth Cragg).[3]

The three quotations above sum up the distinctive features of
three different ways in which Muslims and Christians have
talked together about each other's faith for the last fourteen
hundred years. The words of Robert Holcot in the fourteenth
century provide a justification for *polemics*, which can be defined as attacking another faith with a view to discrediting it.
Temple Gairdner, who worked as a missionary of the Church
Missionary Society in Cairo from 1897 to 1928, is an example
of someone who believed in the need for *apologetics*, which
involves giving a reasoned defence of one's own faith, and
where appropriate challenging the other faith. Kenneth Cragg
summed up the essence of *dialogue* in words addressed to

Muslims and Christians taking part in the World Council of
Churches Chambésy Consultation in 1976.

It is not always possible, however, to draw a hard and fast
line between these three activities. Some apologetics can contain
elements of polemic, while others renounce polemics altogether. Gairdner, as an apologist, hardly ever engaged in polemics; and in the regular public debates he held with sheiks of
the Al-Azhar University, he was probably practising dialogue
more effectively than some who only talk *about* dialogue today.

We shall explore nine examples of exchanges between
Christians and Muslims at different periods of history and in
different contexts, and reflect on some of the issues they raise
for Christians and Muslims in the West today who want to
explore each other's faith.

1. Muhammad's dialogue with a deputation of Christians from Najran

A detailed account of this meeting is found in the *Life of the
Prophet* by Ibn Ishaq (707–73).[4] It tells how, in the year AD 632,
only a few months before the death of the Prophet, a high-
powered delegation consisting of 60 people came from Najran
to Medina to meet the Prophet, led by their chief advisor, an
administrator and a scholar–bishop. The Christians were allowed to pray facing east in the Prophet's mosque in Medina,
and at the very end of the meeting they asked Muhammad to
send someone to sort out certain financial disputes in their
community in Najran. While Ibn Ishaq's account gives a very
Islamic interpretation of the events, with ideas put into the
mouth of the Christians which come from the Qur'an (for
example Jesus speaking from the cradle and the miracle of
creating birds out of clay), there is a great deal that rings true
in the story.

The following observations about the discussion that took
place highlight certain issues which have been relevant in
dialogue between Christians and Muslims at many periods of
history:

(a) The Christians point to the virgin birth as evidence for the divinity of Christ, but find that this is totally unconvincing to the Muslims.

(b) The Christians use the well-known argument about the plural verbs used of God in the Qur'an (for example 'we have done', 'we have commanded') as evidence for the trinity, but find that it carries no weight with the Muslims.

(c) The fundamental concern of the Muslims about Jesus being called 'Son of God' is that it compromises the transcendence and unity of God, which must for the Muslims be safeguarded and defended at all costs.

(d) The basic stumbling block for Muslims is the incarnation. How is it conceivable that the eternal God could die? If Jesus was Almighty God, why could he not do *anything* he wanted to while he was on earth? Why was he still limited in certain ways?

(e) Muhammad invited the Christians to become Muslims, but they declined the invitation. Finally he challenged the Christians to resort to a 'mutual invocation of a curse', probably an ordeal by fire (*mubahala*), something that seems to be referred to in Q. 3:61. Again the Christians declined. If we ask whether they were right to do so, Christians today are divided in their response. Some would argue that Muhammad's challenge presented the opportunity for a decisive 'power encounter'. They had nothing to lose, and following the example of Elijah in his encounter with the priests of Baal on Mount Carmel, could have vindicated their claims for the gospel. Others would see such a response as being unnecessarily provocative. Acceptance of the Christian faith based solely on supernatural phenomena rather than on intellectual and spiritual conviction could hardly be genuine.

(f) The Muslim perception is that these Christians knew in their hearts that Muhammad was a prophet sent by God, but felt they had to remain Christians because they were in the pay of Byzantium. They knew that if they renounced their faith, their financial support would be cut off. Even at this early stage it is evident that politics and religion were closely intertwined!

2. St John of Damascus (675–753)

St John is important in this survey because he was probably
the first Christian we know of who was in close contact with
Islam and who tried to think theologically about Islam and to
teach Christians about their response to the challenge. He was
born 43 years after the death of Muhammad, into a family
which had occupied high positions in government in Damascus for many years. He himself worked in the Ministry of
Finance until the age of fifty, when he retired, perhaps because
of political pressure, to a monastery near Jerusalem, in order
to devote his time to writing. He must have lived and worked
alongside Muslims until the time of his retirement, and therefore had reasonably accurate knowledge of the Qur'an and of
Muslim beliefs and practices.

There are two chapters in John's writings concerning Islam:
a chapter in a book about heresies, *The Heresy of the Ishmaelites*,
and *A Dialogue between a Christian and a Saracen*.[5] One of the
reasons why his work was (and still is) significant is that he
initiated some of the approaches to Islam which were continued by later generations of Christians.

John treated Islam as a Christian heresy, rather than as a
religion in its own right. This was understandable, since he
probably thought Islam was a passing heresy that would not
survive for very long. It meant, however, that he was constantly comparing Islam with Christianity, and therefore
hardly able to think himself into the minds of Muslims. This
issue is still highly relevant today, since there are many Christians who continue to think of Islam simply as a Christian
heresy. The danger in this approach is that one tends to focus
on all the areas in which Islam deviates from Christianity, and
therefore fails to understand the special dynamic of the faith
of Islam for Muslims. Daniel Sahas argues that our approach
to Islam today should 'focus our attention on what the Muslims believe; and this viewed not from the standpoint of the
Christian faith, but on what *they* see and confess as being
crucial and essential in their own faith . . . The "conversion" to
which one is called is to take his partner in the dialogue
seriously on his own terms.'[6]

John attempted to challenge Muslims by taking seriously the text of the Qur'an. He points, for example, to the titles that are given to Jesus in the Qur'an, 'Word of God' and 'a spirit from Him', and argues: 'This is what you believe about Jesus. But how can you separate a person's word from the person himself? How can you separate God from his Word?' This line of argument has frequently been used by Christians and is still felt to be quite effective. Without challenging the text of the Qur'an, it encourages Muslims to think more deeply about their interpretation of the text.

John sometimes argues with Muslims on the basis of the Bible. For example, he suggests the following approach in response to a question from a Muslim: 'Let us use your Scripture and my Scripture . . . Your Scripture says . . . And my Gospel says . . .'[7] Unfortunately Christians tended to quote the Bible for centuries without apparently being aware that Muslims generally do not accept Jewish or Christian Scriptures as genuine.

At times John tends to mock Islamic beliefs. He says, for example, that the Qur'an contains 'certain things worthy of ridicule'. He speaks of 'many other marvels, worthy of ridicule', 'many foolish sayings'.[8] This raises the question of whether it is ever right for Christians (or Muslims) to engage in ridicule. It is sometimes argued that if the prophet Isaiah could ridicule the worship of idols, and if Paul could pour scorn on the idea of a god living in a temple made by human hands (Acts 17:24), there is no reason why Christians should not do the same in certain circumstances. Others would reply that when Christians descend to ridiculing the beliefs and practices of Islam, they are simply inviting ridicule in return.

John is critical of what he regards as Muhammad's sexual indulgence. This, as we shall see, was an argument which became part of the standard Christian polemic against Islam for centuries.

He believed that one of the main sources for Muhammad's beliefs was an Arian monk. This was probably the special twist which Christians gave to the story about Muhammad meeting with the monk called Bahira on one of his journeys to Syria, as recorded by Ibn Ishaq.[9] The idea was developed further by

Christians in the East, no doubt as a way of explaining the false teaching of Islam, and it found its way later into the polemic of the Western church.

John used two arguments in particular which became standard apologetic arguments for centuries:

(a) Muhammad cannot have been a true prophet, firstly because his coming was not foretold in the Scriptures, and secondly because he did not work any miracles. It is interesting to see how Muslims responded to these arguments. If at first they felt themselves in a weak position, it didn't take them long to search the Bible to find texts that they could point to as predictions of Muhammad (for example Deut. 18:15, where Moses predicts the coming of 'a prophet like me'; and John 14:16 and 26, where Jesus predicts the coming of the Paraclete). The orthodox teaching about the miraculous was that Muhammad did not work any miracles, but that the Qur'an itself was the greatest miracle of all.

(b) Muhammad was not sincere; he won people over to his teaching 'by a pretence of godliness'. Christians today are divided over the question of Muhammad's sincerity. Some are prepared to believe that he was utterly sincere in all that he said and did, while others would not hesitate to use the word 'imposter', suggesting a deliberate attempt to deceive.

3. Eighth- and ninth-century Muslim–Christian controversy in Arabic

If Western scholars and missionaries ever think that they are the first to have taken seriously the theological challenge of Islam, it is good for them to be reminded that Arabic-speaking Christians living in the middle East after the time of John of Damascus were engaged in an ongoing dialogue with their Muslim neighbours. A recent study of this literature by Mark Swanson,[10] an American theologian living in Egypt, explains the three main reasons for Muslim antipathy to the symbol of the cross and the Christian understanding of the death of Christ during the first centuries after the rise of Islam:

(a) The cross had become a symbol of the victory first of Roman Christians, and then of Byzantine Christians over their enemies, including especially the Muslim world.
(b) Muslims seem to have thought that Christians worshipped the cross in an idolatrous way.
(c) Muslims did not believe that Jesus should be regarded as divine or that he had been crucified.
(d) They could not believe that salvation for the human race depended on the crucifixion of Jesus.

Swanson believes that the view expressed in Muslim texts in this period that 'to confess the crucifixion is to deny the honor in which God holds Christ' is thoroughly consistent with the teaching of the Qur'an:

> Christ . . . was not merely one of God's prophets (*anbiya'*), but also one of God's apostles (*rusul*). The overwhelming witness of the Qur'an is that God . . . cunningly delivers His apostles from the plots of their enemies, so that they may themselves be signs of God's victory and heartening examples for the one in whom God's victory is made especially manifest, Muhammad.[11]

The response of Arabic-speaking theologians and apologists to these Muslim convictions needs to be taken seriously today for two reasons. Firstly, they were clearly in dialogue with Muslims and understood the Muslim objections to their beliefs. Secondly, they made a real attempt to explain the death of Jesus in terms that Muslims could understand, even if they could not accept them. So, for example, they looked for common ground, like belief in law, judgment, resurrection and the life of the world to come. They took Islamic ideas, such as the idea of God as 'the best of deceivers' (Q. 3:54), and developed them by building on the teaching of the early church fathers, but giving it an Islamic slant.

There were four major themes in their writings:

(a) They interpreted the death of Christ as God's victory over
Satan through the exercise of cunning. One obvious weakness of this approach was that they made so much of the
role of Satan that they appeared to give Satan even more
power than Christ himself.

(b) They told the story of the crucifixion, death and resurrection as a divine demonstration of the reality of the final
resurrection of all people. While Muslims believed that
there would be a resurrection at the end of the world, only
Christians could have any certainty of victory over death,
because they could see the resurrection of Jesus as a
foretaste of the general resurrection.

(c) They believed that through his life of perfect obedience
and his death on behalf of sinful people, Christ fulfilled all
the claims of justice against sinners who are guilty of
breaking God's laws. This kind of argument anticipated
the theme developed in the eleventh century by Anselm in
his *Cur Deus Homo*.

(d) Instead of trying to explain the death of Christ, Christians
sometimes concentrated on 'uncompromising *assertion* of
the paradoxes of Christian faith in a crucified Lord . . . the
"true religion" apology, for which the undeniable spread
of the Christian faith *despite* the stumbling block of its
paradoxical teaching is evidence that its success is *not* to
be explained in merely psychological, sociological, or
political terms'.[12]

With the benefit of hindsight, however, it may be possible for
us to point out certain limitations in these responses:

(a) Christian apologists sometimes relied too heavily on the
argument from prophecy. Using ideas developed earlier
in the course of controversy with Jews, they collected
verses from the Jewish Scriptures that they understood as
predictions not only of the fact, but also of the manner of
Jesus' death. As we have already seen in the case of St John
of Damascus, Muslims did not hesitate to use the same
argument to prove that the coming of Muhammad was
predicted in the Old Testament.

(b) Christians were often slow to realize that because Muslims had Scriptures of their own, they were not always impressed with arguments based on the Old Testament.

(c) Some attempted to argue that the crucial Qur'anic text 'they did not kill him, they did not crucify him . . .' (Q. 4:157) could be given a Christian interpretation. The basic weakness in this approach is that it goes against the Islamic consensus over the centuries about the death of Jesus and puts Christians in the position of appearing to tell Muslims the correct interpretation of the Qur'an.

(d) Christians found it hard to develop a convincing rationale for the death of Jesus. Muslims believed that Christians were denying the honour in which Christ is held by God, and could not understand how God could possibly allow Jesus to undergo such a humiliating and shameful death. In this context Christians did not find it easy to explain precisely *how* and *why* the crucifixion of Jesus could lead to a victory over Satan or the redemption of humankind and the forgiveness of sins.

Christians today no doubt have much to learn from this dialogue which, although it took place over a period of two centuries and was highly creative, did not seem to achieve a significant breakthrough in mutual understanding.

4. Medieval polemic

We are dealing here with the sustained attempt of Christians in the West to discredit Islam and to prove that its claims to revelation were false. Over the centuries the church in the West learned something about Islam from the churches of the East – for example from individuals who travelled to the middle East and North Africa, and from the Crusaders – and turned this information into ammunition to use against Islam.

(i) The nature of the polemic

Norman Daniel in his classic *Islam and the West: the Making of an Image*, notes the following significant features of the consensus about Islam that developed in the minds of Christians in the West.

(a) It was largely based on ignorance or inadequate information. Western Christians had little first-hand contact with Muslims or with Muslim writings. The consensus was not based on any real desire to understand. 'Christian polemicists would never allow their opponents to speak for themselves'[13]; 'no sustained effort was made to present argument in terms that Muslims could recognize as their own.'[14]

(b) Arguments would always start from Christian presuppositions. The Qur'an could not be true because it is so different from the Bible. Alternatively the Qur'an would be used to 'prove' the Bible.[15]

> They could not think themselves, even for purposes of argument, into a position that was not based on Scripture. The Qur'an became the object of their ridicule because it was unfamiliar, and the effort to see that that kind of ridicule was applicable by an enemy to their own Scripture beyond them. They were tied to their own tradition and unable to look outside it.[16]

(c) Frequently there was serious misrepresentation. Polemicists manipulated the facts through careful selection, omission, exaggeration, invention or misapplication.[17] In this way they came to invent absurd and ridiculous fantasies about Muslim beliefs and practices.

> At the worst there was the assertion of the fantastic, and its repetition without discrimination; at best there was the selection of only those facts that served the purpose of controversy . . . Even when after some centuries they came to have more accurate knowledge, there must very often have been a deliberate choice of the worst.[18]

In attempting to explain 'the tendency of misconceptions to snowball',[19] Daniel suggests that the end of discrediting Islam seemed to justify the means. 'Christians thought that whatever tended to harm the enemies of truth was likely itself to be true.'[20]

(d) There was a heavy reliance on rational argument, based on confidence in the power of reason to convince unbelievers. 'Much of the literature about Islam seems to consist of debating points triumphantly enunciated and, of course, never answered, because the opponent is absent.'[21]

(e) The polemic seems to have been directed at Christians more than at Muslims. Christian had strong feelings of hatred, suspicion and fear towards Muslims, because Islam had become to them 'the most powerful instrument for the destruction of the Church, and for the loss of souls and provinces, then known'.[22]

> The overwhelming probability is that the public intended by the polemicists was Christian . . . Nearly all the arguments . . . were admirably formulated to uphold faith. They would suitably horrify those who were at a distance from actual Muslims, but they would also fortify those who could not be guarded physically from Islamic realities. All alike would be confirmed in their suspicion and contempt.[23]

(ii) The content of the polemic

There were three main lines in this sustained attack on Islam. Firstly, the person of Muhammad was criticized. The following arguments were used with the intention of discrediting him completely:

(a) The source of his 'revelations' can be attributed to epilepsy or to demonic possession, or to a dove that was trained by Muhammad to eat a grain of corn from his ear. It was widely believed that Muhammad was taught by Christian heretics, and in particular from one Arian monk. This story almost certainly derives from an early Christian elaboration of the account, found in the earliest Muslim sources, of Muhammad's meeting with the monk Bahira.[24]

(b) Some revelations were self-induced in order to justify particular actions, especially Muhammad's marriage to

Zainab, the wife of his adopted son Zaid. Daniel remarks that 'I cannot stress too much the popularity of this story.'[25]

(c) Muhammad was both ambitious and immoral: 'Muhammad was both wicked and human.'[26] He was a 'licentious hypocrite'.[27] 'It seemed very obvious to medieval Christians that Muhammad's behaviour with women alone made it quite impossible that he should have been a prophet.'

(d) Muhammad performed no miracles.

(e) Muhammad imposed Islam by force and violence.

Secondly, Islam was said to be a religion of self-indulgence:

(a) Islam is sexually permissive. Up to 4 wives are allowed and an unlimited number of concubines. This subject 'exercised a theoretical fascination for Christian writers'.[28] Islam was portrayed as 'the religion which endorsed pleasure, almost, perhaps, as a principle of religion'.[29]

(b) Islam gives permission for divorce.

(c) The Islamic paradise is purely sensual: 'It was thought sufficient barely to contrast an eternity of eating, drinking and copulating with the apprehension of beatitude by the intellect.'[30]

Thirdly, the practice of Islam was attacked. While Christians were at times impressed with the virtuous lives of Muslims, they expressed surprise that they practised Christian virtues, but pointed out that they still fell short of Christian standards. The religion of Islam was therefore seen as one of 'vain outward forms', and their rituals and sacraments as 'poor imitations of Christian models' and 'false-sacraments'.[31]

Many Christians reading about this polemic today will experience an acute sense of shame and embarrassment over some of these things that have been said by Christians to Muslims in the past. While it would not be hard to find more than a trace of this kind of polemic in some of the books about Islam written by (and for) Christians today, there has been a dramatic change in the way most Christian missionaries have written about Islam in recent decades.[32]

5. St Francis (1182–1226)

After two unsuccessful attempts to go to Syria, Spain or Morocco in 1212 and 1213, St Francis finally succeeded in going
to Egypt in 1219. He joined up with the Crusader army at
Damietta, and during a lull in the fighting went over to speak
to the Fatimid Sultan Malik al-Kamil, nephew of the great
Saladin. One of the problems we have with this story is the
difficulty of separating fact from fiction. The original account
is found in a letter by Jacques de Vitry, Bishop of Acre, who
was present at Damietta. But the story has been elaborated
considerably since then.[33]

St Francis is important for this survey because he not only
developed a new approach to the Muslim world, but also communicated his vision to the Franciscan order, so that during and
after his lifetime a number of Franciscans went as missionaries to
different Muslim areas. As a result, writes Jean-Marie Gaudeul,
'the Church in Europe was brought to the realization that God
himself was calling it to a new missionary response among
Muslims'.[34] It is significant that in the *First Rule* which he drew up
for the Order in 1221, he outlined two kinds of missionary approach: the first a Christian presence with a *silent* witness, and the
second, *verbal* proclamation of the gospel, but only 'when they
discern it to be God's will'.

While Christians today must recognize the significance of
the way in which St Francis challenged popular Christian
attitudes towards Islam, they must at the same time acknowledge certain limitations in the approach developed by him
and his successors.

(a) His repudiation of the Crusades was not as strong as is
    sometimes supposed. He did not oppose fighting, and did
    not repudiate the warfare of the Crusades. Benjamin Kedar
    believes that Francis probably thought of his preaching 'as
    a supplementary rather than a contradictory alternative to
    the crusade'.[35] 'Missionary preaching to the Muslims did
    not evolve out of criticism of the Crusades . . . But the
    moving force behind the emergence of sustained preach-
    ing to the Muslims was the urge to bring the Gospel to all

men . . . Preaching to the Muslims was an extension of preaching to the Christians.'[36]

When asked why Christians fought Muslims, Francis replied: 'If your eye offends you, pluck it out and fling it away. So root out utterly him who tries to turn us from faith in God. Therefore Christians invade your land, for you blaspheme the name of Christ.'[37] Norman Daniel recognizes that 'the actual passage to the East of so many friars created a new and important element in the Christian consciousness', but believes that 'missionary thought did not replace the old Crusading ways of thinking'.[38] There was still an uncomfortably close connection between the concepts of 'crusade' and 'mission'.

(b) There was frequently an element of deliberate provocation in the Franciscan approach. They often chose to preach in the open air and sometimes even in mosques, and did not hesitate to attack Muslim beliefs. This was the commission with which they were sent out by St Francis: 'My children, God bade me send you to the land of the Saracens to preach and proclaim his faith and to attack Muhammad's law . . .'[39] They expected immediate results from their preaching, and were disappointed when they did not achieve them.

(c) The Franciscans often actively sought martyrdom. Before St Francis' journey to Egypt, he had sent a party of missionaries to Spain and Morocco, who even before they set out expressed their expectation that they would become martyrs. Underneath this desire was 'a state of mind that could tolerate no relation between Christendom and Islam save that of violence exerted or undergone'.[40] Kedar believes that their longing for martyrdom outweighed the desire to convert Muslims, 'and led them . . . to publicly assail Islam and thus bring death upon themselves'.[41] In yearning for death for themselves, the martyrs were also hoping for 'the death and damnation of the infidels'.[42]

The work of Franciscan missionaries to Muslims resulted in 'evident, striking failure'. This is the evaluation of Jean-Marie Gaudeul, himself a Catholic:

The approach of the Franciscans, as it developed in the 200 years after the death of St. Francis, did not achieve significant positive results. These violent deaths often marked the end, temporary or definitive, of the mission in a given region and the loss of any good will which may have existed between Christians and Muslims before the events.

More than any other factor, this failure gave credit to the idea that 'nothing could be done among Muslims'. Gradually, the ideals of 'evangelisation of Muslims' were abandoned as impractical, impossible.[43]

It was not long before they realized that they needed to change their strategy:

Within a century or two, the main purpose of the Franciscans' presence in Muslim lands had become that of looking after the foreign Christians (traders, pilgrims, soldiers, captives) and guarding Christian sanctuaries . . . This 'exemplary' failure made other thinkers express the idea that Mission among Muslims could only succeed if political power was in Christian or neutral hands, so that conversions would not be hampered by social pressure, or sanctioned by martyrdom . . .[44]

In spite of all these limitations, Kenneth Cragg wants to point to the inspiration that Christians today can still derive from St Francis' special concern for the Muslim world:

'Interpretation' across the frontiers of assumption and dogma seems to have been impossible. It was the gesture of the saint in incurring the rough handling the Fatimid soldiers gave him which articulated the Christian will for contact . . . Transit from 'camp to camp' is so different in our day when the possibilities of intelligent exchange, not to say personal relationship, are so much readier than in that embattled, medieval day. But the Franciscan 'marks of Jesus' (Gal. 6:17) will always be the making of the 'instruments of his peace'.[45]

6. Raymond Lull (1235–1315)

The life of Raymond Lull, who was of Spanish birth and born in Majorca, seems to hold a special fascination for evangelical Christians. Samuel Zwemer's sympathetic study of his life was published in 1902. The popular study course *Ishmael My Brother* includes a chapter on his life and work that gives a generally positive view of his achievements.[46] From our perspective today the positive aspects of his approach can be listed as follows:

(a) He questioned the Crusades. In the words of Cragg, 'he courageously repudiated the physical belligerence of the Crusading instinct and insisted that it must be replaced by genuine compassion and scholarly evangelism'.[47]
(b) He took seriously the need for study and thorough preparation, recognizing the importance of knowing Arabic and mastering local languages. He set up his own missionary training college in Majorca in 1276, and spent much time lobbying in the Vatican for the setting up of faculties for teaching Arabic and Islam.
(c) He was a great writer, with a total of two hundred published books and pamphlets.
(d) He practised what he preached about engaging in mission to Muslims.
(e) His mission was inspired by a deep spirituality and a spirit of self-sacrifice. 'There is but one way of conquest,' he wrote, 'namely by love and prayers, and the pouring out of tears and blood. For he who loves not lives not . . .'[47]

There are certain limitations in Lull's approach, however, some of which are not discussed in popular accounts of his life.

(a) Being a child of his age, he was not able to free himself entirely from the mentality of the Crusades. While he questioned the Crusades and called for an alternative approach to Islam, his concept of Christian mission still included many elements of the Crusades of his day. He believed, for example, that as long as Muslims controlled the land it would be impossible to convert them, and that the only way to convert Muslims would be to bring them under Christian power.[48] If they could not be brought under Christian power, it was necessary to 'fight them and expel them from the land which is ours by right'.

Words like the following certainly protest strongly against the methods of the crusaders, but do not really seem to challenge their goal of regaining political control of Palestine:

> Many knights I see going to the Holy Land to conquer it by force of arms. But looking to the result of it, all give up before they fulfil their desire. It seems to me, therefore, O Lord, that the Holy Land will never be conquered except by love and prayer and the shedding of tears as well as blood. Let the knights go forth adorned with the sign of the Cross and filled with the grace of the Holy Spirit, and preach the truth concerning Thy passion.[49]

Kedar believes that it is possible to trace a gradual hardening of Lull's attitudes during his lifetime. At the age of thirty-six, in 1271 he called for 'the conquest of the Holy Land as Jesus did'.[50] Ten years later he wrote that the emperor should wage war on infidels if they refuse to listen to preaching but that they should not be converted against their will.[51]

In 1291 he seemed to place crusade in the service of mission,[52] and contemplated the possibility of enforced instruction.[53] By 1305 he was speaking of offering incentives to Muslim converts,[54] and in 1308 he even suggested plans for a crusade that could begin with a naval attack. In his last work in 1314 there is a clear affirmation of crusades to defend the Roman Church against 'the infidels who hold the Holy Land'.[55]

(b) Lull was supremely confident in the power of reason. He believed that nothing was beyond the range of reason, and that all that is required to defend Christianity before Muslims is good reasoning. He was confident that rational proof could be found for every doctrine, including the trinity and incarnation. He thought of one of his major apologetic works, *Ars agna*, as 'an instrument' by which he conceived it would be possible 'to provide answers to all rational questions'.[56] As a result of this confidence, 'Lull felt perpetually teased by the wilfulness or stupidity of Muslims who could not understand and would not accept what he had once explained to them.'[57]

(c) He was unnecessarily provocative. In his preaching in Bujaya during one of his visits to north Africa, the thrust of his message was that 'the law of the Christians is holy and true, and the sect of the Moors is false and wrong . . .'[58]

Some estimates of Lull's life and work from the perspective of the twentieth century have been critical of his achievements. Sweetman, for example, the author of the classic *Islam and Christian Theology*, writes: 'What there is of permanent value in the intellectual travail of Raymond Lull is extremely doubtful.'[59] Benjamin Kedar refers to parts of what Lull wrote in a book shortly before his death and comments:

> The old man, now well in his eighties, at last gives up his attempts to propagate crusade and mission at the gates of the great of Catholic Europe, and decides in a final, possibly desperate act to hurl at the Saracens the not-inconsiderable force of his intellect, perhaps also the ultimate testimony to his faith. The speech of Justice proves that he did not come to renounce the crusade; he merely decided to retreat to the one course of action upon which he could embark without outside assistance.[60]

Once again Cragg is kinder in his evaluation:

> 'Raymond Lull was squarely with his time yet splendidly transcending it . . . His deepest creation of love was his own lonely and insistent heroism in Tunis, defying deportation and ridicule and finally almost courting martyrdom as, to his mind, the ultimate gesture of Christ's devotion. Centuries elapsed before his real meaning found emulation.'[61]

7. Karl Gottlieb Pfander (1803–65)

In a history of the Church Missionary Society published in 1898 Pfander was described as 'the greatest of all missionaries to Mohammedanism'. He was a German who, after 12 years of work in Istanbul, moved to India in 1837. His famous apologetic work, *Balance of Truth*, was written originally in German in 1829, when Pfander was 26. The latest Arabic and English editions were published around 1986.[62]

On 10 and 11 April 1854 he held two public debates in Agra with a Muslim scholar named Maulana Rahmatullah al-Kairanawi. It appears that the debates were called for by the Muslim community, which felt threatened by the impact of British imperialism and Christian mission. While many Christians hailed the debate as a victory, the Muslim verdict on the debate was that Pfander 'suffered a humiliating defeat'.[63] His opponent in the debate later wrote *Izhar-ul-Haqq* (*Truth Revealed*), first published in Arabic in 1864, the book that has been called 'the first great classic of modern Muslim polemics',[64] and was translated into English in 1900.[65]

The strengths of Pfander's work can be summarized briefly. Firstly, he knew a great deal about Islam and could quote from the Qur'an, the *hadith* and from other Muslim sources in different languages. Secondly, his style was courteous and polite. Thirdly, he could recognize common ground between Christian and Muslim beliefs.

Once again, with the benefit of hindsight, we need also to recognize some of the weaknesses and limitations of Pfander's approach.

(a) His attacks sometimes degenerated into polemics. His criticism of Muhammad, for example, sometimes resulted in tit-for-tat criticism of Christ by Muslims. Bevan Jones, a Baptist missionary who worked in India for many years, was aware of the considerable effect of the kind of approach represented by Pfander: 'Much of the bitterly anti-Christian literature (though by no means all of it) that has issued of late from the Muslim side has been directly provoked by the anti-Muslim books and pamphlets of an earlier generation of Christian writers.'[66]

(b) Pfander appealed too much to the reason and the intellect, and not enough to the heart. The debate could hardly be an open-ended discussion, because he himself had decided from the beginning the criteria by which genuine revelation is to be determined.

(c) He was also unaware of developments in biblical criticism and theology in the West. He was helpless when his Muslim protagonist showed that he knew more about these subjects than he did. Christine Schirrmacher suggests that the debate 'marked a turning point in Muslim apologetics, for it was probably the first time that Muslim theologians used European critical methods to disprove Christian belief.'[67]

(d) It could be argued that Pfander's general approach was more conditioned by the social and political context in which he worked than he realized. He lived under the British Raj in India, and could rely on the protection and support of the British rulers. In the eyes of Muslims Pfander's Christianity would have been identified with the oppression and exploitation of colonial rule. It was only three years after the great debate, in 1857, that the anger of Indian Muslims erupted in what Indians now call the War of Independence, and which the British have called 'the Indian Mutiny'. Pfander's approach expresses the confidence of an apologist whose position in society is thoroughly secure. An Egyptian Copt could hardly have written in this way during the time of Nasser, and a Malaysian Christian in the 1990s could never dare to challenge Islam in the way that Pfander did.

(e) We may today want to question the value of public debates of this kind, which concentrate entirely on purely theological issues and ignore the many social and political issues in the context in which Muslims and Christians are living together.

(f) If one of the major weapons in the Muslim armoury is to attack the Bible, Christians feel compelled to defend the Bible against these attacks and to argue for the divine authority of Scripture. As long as Muslims point to an infallible Qur'an, many Christians feel they want to point to an infallible Bible. Christians who respond in this way, however, find themselves answering Muslims in *their* terms, on *their* ground. Since it is generally the Muslims who take the initiative in the debate and attack the Bible, the Christians are inevitably forced onto the defensive, and have to respond to the challenge in the terms that are offered. So if Christians concede that there is the slightest error in the Bible (for example over the numbers in Kings and Chronicles), they seem to have conceded that their Scriptures cannot be infallible.

By arguing over Scripture in this way, therefore, Christians are allowing the debate to become, as it were, a contest between two infallible Scriptures. They are encouraging Muslims to think that Christians think of Scripture in the same way as Muslims do. If the Qur'an is the very words of God recited by the Prophet, surely the Bible must be regarded as being inspired in the same way. This presents a problem for Muslim readers when they find that the Bible looks so different from the Qur'an. If Christians allow themselves to be drawn into such a contest of two competing Scriptures, it may be even harder in the long run to explain that there is a fundamental difference between the two faiths in their understanding of how God reveals himself to humankind. While Muslims believe that the supreme revelation of God has come in the form of a book, the Qur'an, Christians believe that his supreme revelation has come in the form of a person, Jesus.

The Muslim response to Pfander in *Izhar-ul-Haqq* has certainly provided subsequent generations of Muslims with 'a sort of apologetic encyclopedia'.[68] But it also raises important questions about the role of apologetics in dialogue.

8. The Chambésy Consultation

The main papers from this consultation on *Christian Mission and Islamic* Da'wah, which was held in June 1976 at Chambésy in Switzerland, were first published in the *International Review of Mission* in 1976, and later published as a separate volume by the Islamic Foundation in Leicester. The theme of the consultation was the concept and practice of mission and *da'wa*. Of particular interest in the context of this chapter are the exchanges that took place between Kenneth Cragg and Isma'il al-Faruqi on four particular issues.

(i)   The meaning of revelation

Al-Faruqi states the traditional orthodox understanding of divine revelation in an uncompromising way:

> God does *not* reveal Himself. He does not reveal Himself to anyone in any way. God reveals only His will . . . Christians talk about the revelation of God Himself – by God of God – but that is the great difference between Christianity and Islam. God is transcendent, and once you talk about self-revelation you have hierophancy and immanence, and then the transcendence of God is compromised. You may not have complete transcendence and self-revelation at the same time.

Cragg responds by suggesting that al-Faruqi's Islamic understanding of complete transcendence is hardly consistent with the idea of creation: 'The creation of man is an involvement of the divine will with the human answer . . . Theism . . . must mean divine involvement for this . . . is implicit in creation itself.'[69]

(ii)   God's response to human sin

God's way of dealing with sin, according to Faruqi, is to reveal his will in the Qur'an, thus offering humankind a comprehensive law covering every aspect of life: 'Islam recognizes the universality of sin and God deals with it by sending down the Qur'an.' The Christian understanding, according to Cragg, is that law, exhortation and argument are not enough, since 'they may provoke the very disobedience they condemn'.[70]

(iii)   Incarnation

Faruqi is emphatic that incarnation compromises God's transcendence, while Cragg believes that it does not: 'We have a marvellous example of kingship in *Henry V*, when the king lays the crown aside and shows a simple concern to get alongside the common soldier in a dire situation. Is this less kingly than sitting in the Palace on a throne? I think most of us would agree that it is not.'[71]

(iv) Freedom and apostasy

Cragg challenges the traditional understanding of the Law of Apostasy presented by Faruqi with the comment: 'A faith which you are not free to leave becomes a prison, and no self-respecting faith should be a prison for those within it.'[72]

   The transcript of other parts of the Chambesy Consultation illustrates the difficulties that Muslims and Christians often experience when discussing what it has been like to be at the receiving end of the other's mission. But these exchanges between Faruqi and Cragg come nearer than many examples of formal dialogue to practising the kind of dialogue Cragg was calling for, which involves openness at a deep level to what the other is saying.

9. Kenneth Bailey's interpretation of the parables of Jesus

Having spent most of his working life in the middle East, Kenneth Bailey, an American scholar, has developed three particular tools for interpreting the parables of Jesus, each of which may shed some light on the way in which Christians can communicate their understanding of Jesus to Muslims today. Firstly, his understanding of the poetic structure of much of the teaching of Jesus frequently reveals deeper meaning in the text. Poetry and story may be more powerful means of communication than theological or apologetic literature. Secondly, he believes that the culture still to be found in Egyptian, Palestinian or Lebanese villages is very close to the culture of the time of Jesus, and that such cultural understanding is vital for an understanding of the text. Thirdly, his reading of commentaries on the gospels written by Arabic-speaking Christians gives him access to what was a living tradition developed over many centuries in the Arab East.

Bailey believes that one major theme that runs through many of the parables of Jesus can be summed up in the words: *the costly demonstration of unexpected love*. Each of the four main words is important:

(a) God *loves* all people.
(b) His love is *unexpected*, since we would not expect him to love his rebellious creatures.
(c) Not only does he proclaim his love, however, he actually *demonstrates* his love in action.
(d) This demonstration of his unexpected love is *costly* for him, since in a sense he suffers in the process of forgiving sins.

He finds all these themes developed in an especially powerful way in the parable of the prodigal son, which he sees as the parable of the two lost sons. The father loves his sons, both the rebellious one who wants to leave home and the older one who has a cold and formal relationship with him. He goes on loving them, even when we might expect him to want to punish and reject them. He demonstrates his love to both of them in ways that would have been considered surprising, if not shocking, to his original hearers. And he suffers in the process of demonstrating his love for them. Bailey summarizes the significance of the prodigal's homecoming as follows:

> On his return, the prodigal is overwhelmed by an unexpected visible demonstration of love in humiliation. He is shattered by the offer of grace, confesses unworthiness, and accepts restoration to sonship in genuine humility. Sin is now a broken relationship which he cannot restore. Repentance is now understood as acceptance of grace and confession of unworthiness. The community rejoices together. The visible demonstration of love in humiliation is seen to have clear overtones of the atoning work of Christ.[73]

If it seems strange to include Bailey's work in this context, there are reasons for believing that this parable could be particularly valuable for conveying something of the Christian gospel to the Muslim mind. Muslims are taught to think of themselves as 'servants' who relate to God as their 'master'. So when the

Prodigal thinks of coming home, his face-saving plan is that he will ask his father to accept him back as a servant or slave, so that he can earn his wages and at least have something to pay back to his father. Such a solution, however, is unthinkable to his father, who wants to welcome him home as a son. Jesus, who spoke of himself as 'the Son' who enjoyed an especially intimate relationship with God as Father, brought the good news that all his disciples can approach God as Father and have all the privileges and responsibilities of being full members of God's family, and not just servants. Moreover if Muslims find it hard to understand explanations of the death of Jesus in terms of theological propositions like those of the earlier Arab apologists, can this vivid and unforgettable picture of the father running through the village and welcoming his son home convey in some small way the idea of a God who takes upon himself all the consequences of human rebellion and sin, who actually (dare we say?) suffers in the process of coming to meet us, and who restores us to the kind of relationship for which we were created?

Conclusion

A brief survey of this kind may remind us that we are heirs to a long tradition, and that many others have trodden these paths before us. We are not in the business of criticizing those who have gone before from the vantage point of our superior wisdom. But we do want to stand on their shoulders and work with determination for a greater degree of mutual understanding.

We must be aware of the particular context in which we meet. In every situation either Christians or Muslims or both will feel that there are issues in the context which need to be addressed and talked through. Often there will be deep pain and anger which need to be expressed. The challenge is to find ways of expressing that pain and anger, but at the same time to rise above them and to reach out in genuine friendship.

Christians and Muslims need to meet each other first and foremost as people. We need to meet not so much as representatives of two great world religions, but as Muhammad and John, Fatima and Jean. We need to be willing to engage with each other with openness and vulnerability, and to share at the level of the heart as much as the head. In many situations it seems that women are far more effective than men in establishing this kind of dialogue.

We need to learn from methods of the past which have proved ineffective. Is it too much to hope, for example, that polemics can be ruled out on both sides? While there is ample scope both for Christians and Muslims in defending their faith and challenging the other, there cannot be much respect, let alone love, if the aim is to destroy and discredit the faith of the other.

We need to be transparent in our motives. Muslims are often suspicious of the motives of Christians who engage in dialogue, fearing that the initiative is aimed at proselytization. Christians, on the other hand, can be equally suspicious of the real motives of Muslims who engage in politics of different kinds. While some believe that there cannot be any genuine dialogue whenever one partner has any secret desire to change the mind of the other, many others would say that the most enriching kind of dialogue takes place between people who are so passionate about what they believe that they want to share it with others.

We cannot ignore contemporary political and social issues. We cannot conduct our debates or dialogue as if we live in an ivory tower. The following three chapters should at least make the point that dialogue doesn't have to be about theology at all. Whether we are talking about human rights, education or things to do with church and state, there is still the real possibility of a meeting of hearts and minds.

Notes

[1] Quoted in Benjamin Kedar, *Crusade and Mission: European approaches towards the Muslims*, Princeton University Press, 1984, p. 202.

[2] Constance Padwick, *Temple Gairdner of Cairo*, SPCK, London, 1929, p. 148.

3   Kenneth Cragg, 'Christian Mission and Islamic Da'wah', in *Proceedings of the Chambésy Dialogue Consultation*, The Islamic Foundation, Leicester, 1982, p. 49.
4   A. Guillaume, *The Life of Muhammad: A Translation of Ibn Ishaq's Sirat Rasul Allah*, Oxford University Press, 1955, p. 270ff.
5   Translation by John W. Voorhis, *Muslim World*, vol. 24, 1934, pp. 391–8, and *Muslim World*, vol. 25, 1935, pp. 266–73.
6   Daniel J. Sahas, *John of Damascus on Islam: The heresy of the Ishmaelites*, E.J. Brill, Leiden, 1972, pp. 129–30.
7   Voorhis, op. cit., p. 268.
8   Voorhis, op. cit., pp. 392–3.
9   Guillaume, op. cit., pp. 79–81.
10 Mark N. Swanson, *Folly to the Hunafa: The cross of Christ in Arabic Christian-Muslim controversy in the eighth and ninth centuries*, excerpts from a doctoral dissertation at the Pontifical Institute for Arabic and Islamic Studies, Cairo, 1995.
11 Swanson acknowledges his indebtedness over this point to the article by Willem A. Bijlefeld, 'A Prophet and More than a Prophet', in *Muslim World*, vol. 59, 1969, pp. 1–28.
12 Swanson, op. cit., pp. 13–14.
13 Norman Daniel, *Islam and the West: The making of an image*, Edinburgh University Press, 1980, p. 57.
14 Ibid., p. 193.
15 Ibid., pp. 23–4.
16 Ibid., p. 77.
17 Ibid., p. 242.
18 Ibid.
19 Ibid., p. 243.
20 Ibid., p. 245.
21 Ibid., p. 256.
22 Ibid., p. 245.
23 Ibid., p. 263.
24 Guillaume, op. cit., pp. 79–82.
25 Daniel, op. cit., p. 98.
26 Ibid., p. 96.
27 Ibid., p. 102.
28 Ibid., p. 137.
29 Ibid., p. 269.
30 Ibid., p. 149.

31 Ibid., p. 227.
32 See Kate Zebiri, *Muslims and Christians Face to Face*, One World, Oxford, 1997, Chapter 3.
33 Jean-Marie Gaudeul, *Encounters and Clashes: Islam and Christianity in history*, Pontifical Institute for Arabic and Islamic Studies, Rome, 1984, vol. 1, pp. 151ff.
34 Ibid., p. 151.
35 Kedar, op. cit., p. 131.
36 Ibid., pp. 133–4.
37 Ibid., p. 157.
38 Daniel, op. cit., p. 118.
39 Gaudeul, op. cit., p. 155.
40 Daniel, op. cit., p. 122.
41 Kedar, op. cit., p. 125.
42 Ibid., p. 126.
43 Gaudeul, op. cit., p. 156.
44 Ibid.
45 Kenneth Cragg, *Having in Remembrance: A calendar of middle East saints*, Jerusalem and Middle East Church Association, no date, p. 9.
46 Anne Cooper, *Ishmael my Brother*, 2nd Edition, MARC Europe, Send the Light and Evangelical Missionary Alliance, 1993, pp. 214–16.
47 Quoted in Cragg, op. cit., p. 11.
48 Daniel, op. cit., pp. 118–19.
49 Quoted in Sweetman, *Islam and Christian Theology*, Lutterworth, London, 1945, vol 3, p. 113.
50 Kedar, op. cit., p. 190.
51 Ibid., p. 192.
52 Ibid., p. 195.
53 Ibid., p. 196.
54 Ibid.
55 Ibid., pp. 198–9.
56 Sweetman, op. cit., p. 96.
57 Daniel, op. cit., p. 180.
58 Ibid., p. 121.
59 Sweetman, op. cit., p. 104.
60 Kedar, op. cit., p. 199.
61 Cragg, op. cit., p. 11.

62 C.G. Pfander, *Mizanu'l Haqq (Balance of Truth)*, The Religious Tract Society, London, 1910; reprinted by.

63 Syed Abul Hasan Ali Nadwi, *Da'wah in the West: The Qur'anic Paradigm*, The Islamic Foundation, Leicester, 1992, p. 15.

64 Harry Gaylard Dorman, *Towards Understanding Islam*, Edinburgh, 1948, quoted in Christine Schirrmacher, 'Muslim Apologetics and the Agra Debate of 1854: A nineteenth century turning point', *Bulletin*, Henry Martyn Institute, Hyderabad, Jan–June 1994, p. 77. See further Ann Avril Powell, 'Maulana Rahmat Allah Kairanawi and Muslim-Christian Controversy in India in the Middle 19th Century', *Journal of the Royal Asiatic Society*, vol. 20, 1976; also her unpublished PhD thesis from the University of London, *Contest and Controversy between Islam and Christianity in Northern India 1833–1857: The relations between Muslims and protestant missionaries in the north-western provinces and Oudh*, 1983.

65 A shorter English version was published in three volumes by Ta Ha Publishers, London, in 1989.

66 Quoted in Clinton Bennett, *Victorian Images of Islam*, Grey Seal, London, 1992, p. 148.

67 Schirrmacher, op. cit., p. 74.

68 Ibid., p. 78.

69 Cragg, op. cit., p. 49.

70 Ibid., pp. 45–6.

71 Ibid., p. 51.

72 Ibid., p. 92.

73 Kenneth E. Bailey, *Poet and Peasant, and Through Peasant Eyes*, Eerdmans, Michigan, 1983, p. 206. See also his *Finding the Last: Culture Keys to Luke 15*, Concordia, St. Louis, 1992.

Five

Human Rights: A Conflict between Secular and Islamic Concepts?

Introduction

Muslims experience the tension between the competing norma-tive claims as a kind of collective schizophrenia . . . a truly 'rending' problem for devout Muslims . . . (Schwartländer and Bielefeldt).[1]

Though man has no rights within a theocratic perspective, only duties to his Maker, these duties in their turn give rise to all the rights (A.K. Brohi).[2]

God alone is the real sovereign . . . God is the real law-giver and the authority of absolute legislation vests in Him . . . An Islamic state must, in all respects, be founded upon the law laid down by God through His Prophet (Abul Ala Mawdudi).[3]

The lack of support for the principle of freedom of religion in the Islamic human rights schemes is one of the factors that most sharply distinguishes them from the International Bill of Human Rights, which treats freedom of religion as an unqualified right (Ann Elizabeth Mayer).[4]

If Arab proclamations of adherence to the universal 'idea of human rights' – and indeed, if protests by Arab states against the human rights records of other, non-Arab states – are meant to be taken seriously, then a reconciliation of Islamic and international law must be undertaken. The question is whether such a recon-ciliation can be accomplished without the complete rejection or reconstruction of Islamic law (Donna E. Arzt).[5]

The issue of human rights is one in which there appear at first
sight to be fundamental differences between Islamic values
and those that have developed in the West in recent years.
Some Muslims see no need to adopt the language of human
rights, believing that it springs from thoroughly secular ways
of thinking that have no place in Islam. Others, however, have
no difficulty in entering the debate, and are confident that
these newer ways of thinking can easily be justified in terms
of basic Islamic values.

In this chapter we begin by recognizing the concerns that
Christians, especially in the West, bring to the debate. We then
go on to explore basic concepts about human rights in Islam,
and try to pin-point the main areas of tension between Islam and
secular ways of thinking. We soon find that the debate highlights some fundamental issues at stake, and reveals the wide
spectrum of views within Islam, including many calls for the
reform of Islamic law to bring it more closely into line with
international law as it is understood in the West.

1. Christians and human rights

If we ask why human rights is a subject of particular concern
for Christians (especially in the West) in their thinking about
Islam, it needs to be admitted that for many it arises largely
out of a concern for Muslim converts to Christianity. These
individuals are often rejected by their families, lose their jobs,
are disinherited and even divorced, interrogated or impris-
oned by the police, forced to leave their community and their
country, and sometimes even killed. Mehdi Dibaj, for example, an Iranian Christian from a Muslim background, was
brutally murdered in Tehran early in 1994 simply because he
was considered guilty in the eyes of many Muslims of the
crime of apostasy. According to these Muslims he had to be
executed in obedience to a fundamental principle enshrined
in traditional Islam law, which has been summarized by
Abdallah An-Naim, a Sudanese professor of law now resi-
dent in the USA, as follows: 'According to all the established
schools of Islamic jurisprudence, as accepted by the vast

majority of Muslims today, an apostate must be put to death, his property confiscated, and his Muslim wife divorced from him, regardless of her wishes.'[6]

If this is a major part of the agenda for Christians who are concerned about human rights in the Islamic world, it is especially important that they attempt to see the issue within a broader context and with some kind of historical perspective. Taking time to see the question of human rights in this context should perhaps encourage them to enter the debate with greater caution.

(a) The question of apostasy needs to be seen in the context of the wider debate about Islam and human rights. If Christians, for example, focus on the position of Christian minorities in Muslim countries, are they aware of the problems faced by other minorities like the Ahmadis or the Bahai? And are they aware of a whole range of other issues concerning human rights in the Muslim world, like the position of women, slavery, freedom of the press, repressive government and so forth? Kevin Dwyer's book *Arab Voices: The human rights debate in the middle East* is an excellent study of a wide range of issues, and a valuable reminder of the wider range of human rights issues in that part of the world.[7]
(b) The acceptance of human rights is a relatively recent development. The first clear statements of human rights in the Western world came in the Virginia Bill of Rights in 1776 and the French *Declaration des droits de l'homme and du citoyen* in 1798. After the religious wars of the sixteenth century and slavery in the eighteenth and nineteenth centuries and the excesses of capitalism, imperialism, Fascism, Nazism and Communism in the twentieth century, the Western world became painfully aware of the need to protect individuals from oppressive powers of one kind or another. 'It was because of such experiences of structural injustice,' says Heiner Bielefeldt, 'that the concept of human rights gradually took shape. *Specifically modern threats to human life and dignity had made necessary specifically modern safeguards . . .*'[8]

(c) Christians should not imagine that they can easily find a charter for human rights in the Bible! Mohamed Talbi, in an article entitled 'Religious Liberty: A Muslim perspective', describes the position of the Jews in the Old Testament period, thinking particularly of passages like Deuteronomy 13:1–18 and Leviticus 24:10–16, and makes the following comment:

> It is the perfect prototype of an ethnically homogeneous community, rooted in religion and shaped into a land and a state. In a way, to speak of religious liberty in such a case is literally absurd. There is no choice other than remaining in the State–Community or leaving it. In particular the Jew who is converted to another religion ceases *ipso facto* to belong to his State– Community. So his conversion is felt as a betrayal and, as such, it warrants the penalty of death.[9]

Although some may be confident that they can find a clear basis in Scripture for the concept of human dignity, 'human rights in the sense of universal rights of equal freedom and participation', as Bielefeldt points out, 'are unknown in the Bible which accepts even slavery as a social reality and a legal institution'.[10] In all the three Abrahamic religions, therefore, apostasy has generally been seen in the past as 'a public act of religious and social dissent which cuts its perpetrator off from the community socially and spiritually, if not physically'.[11]

(d) It is only comparatively recently that Christians in the West have accepted the concept of human rights wholeheartedly. It was long seen by Christians as 'alien and detrimental to the Christian ethics of love, charity and mutual care', and leading to 'a *secular* concept of law, politics and state. In the opinion of many theologians and church leaders, religious liberty came close to agnosticism and atheism.'[12] Although individual Christians were involved in formulating the first declarations, the leaders of both Protestant and Catholic Churches were largely unconvinced until the present century. And it was only in the late 1960s that the Roman Catholic Church finally endorsed the idea of religious liberty at the Second Vatican Council.[13]

(e) It is hardly possible to argue that Christianity can take all the credit for the development of human rights. 'It has to be admitted,' says Bielefeldt, 'that human rights do not simply derive from the Christian tradition in its entirety. They are at least not a "natural" or "self-evident" result of that tradition.'[14] He therefore warns against the temptation of 'the "dialectical reappropriation" of human rights into Christian theology and tradition'.[15] Both Christians and Muslims reached this same conclusion at a conference in Tunis in 1982. Their report recognized that 'the philosophical elaboration of the notion of "human rights" has taken place without reference to the spirit of the Gospel or to the ethic of the Qur'an. Everything has transpired as if human rights issued entirely from a single source of "natural" principles, and as if faith in man alone could guarantee the respect of human dignity.'[16] Mahmoud Ayoub goes further when he says it can be argued 'that freedom of religion as an ideal is the child of the twin-phenomenon of the decline of religion and the rise of individualism in Western culture'.[17]

(f) Christians need to admit that historically Islam probably has a better record of toleration than Christianity. In the words of Ann Elizabeth Mayer in *Islam and Human Rights: Tradition and politics*, an important study which will be quoted frequently in this chapter, 'despite incidents of discrimination and mistreatment of non-Muslims, it is fair to say that the Muslim world, when judged by the standards of the day, generally showed far greater tolerance and humanity in its treatment of religious minorities than did the Christian West.'[18]

(g) The perception of Muslims is that people in the West, including Christians, are more influenced by their situation than they realize. They need to listen to three protests in particular. The first is that the media frequently make a connection between violence and Islam, but play down the situations in which it is the state that is responsible for violence. The second is the fact that the West often seems

guilty of hypocrisy and double standards. Why, for example, do they take such interest in individual cases of human
rights but at the same time ignore the human rights of a
whole nation, the Palestinians? Thirdly, the West is often
perceived as using human rights to its own advantage. The
people of the middle East, for example, cannot easily forget
the ways in which Western powers in the past have attempted to interfere in the politics of the area on the pretext
of attempting to support minority communities in their
midst. As a result, says Mayer, 'European expressions of
solicitude for non-Muslims naturally became associated
with hypocrisy and selfish political ambitions.'[19] Similarly
Saif believes that human rights are identified in the eyes
of many with Westernization, cultural alienation and foreign intervention. The West assumes the role of 'the global
custodian of human rights', and uses talk about human
rights as 'yet another implement for the Americanization
of world culture'.

These considerations, taken together, should perhaps encourage a greater humility in the minds of Christians who are
vocal about their concern for human rights in the world of
Islam. Could this perhaps be seen as an area in which 'the
children of this world are wiser . . . than the children of light'
(Luke 16:8 AV)?

2. Basic concepts about human rights in Islam

Both secularists and Christians in the West need to appreciate
some of the basic assumptions which Muslims bring to any
discussion about human rights.

(i) The sovereignty of God

Muslim writers constantly emphasize the fundamentally different starting points for Islamic and secular concepts of human rights: the Islamic approach is theocentric, while the
Western approach is anthropocentric:

Islam presents man with a Charter of Human Liberty within a religious framework which emphasizes the necessity of his being aware of his responsibility and accountability.[20]

What distinguishes the Islamic concept of Human Rights is that these rights were not granted under any threat of political agitation or popular revolt. They were freely and willingly given by God and His Prophet who had nothing to fear from his followers.[21]

(ii) Duties rather than rights

Humankind in Islam is seen as God's vicegerent (*khalifa*) on earth (Q. 2:30), and exists only to serve God. Muslims therefore distinguish between *huquq-Allah*, the rights of God, that is human obligations to God, the demands that God can make of humankind, and *huquq-al'ibad* or *huquq-unnas*, the rights of human beings. Human beings cannot begin to think about their rights until they have accepted their duties towards God, and any rights they have are derived solely from their duties:

> Human rights [in Islam] exist only in relation to human obligations. Individuals possess certain obligations toward God, fellow humans, and nature, all of which are defined in the *Shari'ah*. When individuals meet these obligations they acquire certain rights and freedoms which are again prescribed by the *Shari'ah*. Those who do not accept these obligations have no rights, and any claims of freedom that they make upon society lack justification.[22]

(iii) The rights of individuals within the state

Islam thinks of the individual in the context of his/her total community, while Western secular thinking tends to emphasize the rights of the individual over against the state:

> The individual if necessary has to be sacrificed in order that the life of the organism be saved. Collectivity has a special sanctity attached to it in Islam.[23]

Unlike western philosophical and political perceptions of the separability of the individual and the state, Islamic social concepts do not make such a distinction. The individual does not stand in any adversarial position vis à vis the state but is an integral part thereof. The consequence of this relationship ... is that there is no apparent need to delineate individual rights in contraposition to the state.[24]

The concept of human rights, according to Mayer, is based on 'Western traditions of individualism, humanism, and rationalism and on legal principles protecting individual rights',[25] and has been developed in the West to protect individuals from the coercive power of the state. Such an idea is alien to Islam, where there is no need to protect the rights of the individual over against society in general or the government. 'Scholars of Islamic law ... ,' she writes, 'tended to think of the relationship between ruler and ruled solely in terms of this idealized scheme, in which rulers were conceived of as pious Muslims eager to follow God's mandate. No need was perceived to protect the rights of the individual vis-à-vis society or the government...'[26] Although there are ideas about the equality of individuals within the state, 'one does not find any counterpart of the principle of equal protection under the law'.[27] Brohi believes that 'there can, in the strict theory of Islamic law, be no conflict between the State Authority and the individual – since both have to obey the Divine Law'.[28] The background to these ideas in Islamic legal thinking and practice of the past are explained by Arzt:

> Because of this view that normally the individual and the state stand in a nonadversarial relationship, Islamic constitutionalism does not include the concept of government checks and balances that most Western constitutional scholars have come to believe are essential to the guarantee of human rights. N.J. Coulson has written that because Islamic jurisprudence ideally rejects the possibility of any conflict between the interests of the executive and those of the law, and is premised on the assumption of the ideally qualified ruler, 'no adequate machinery, therefore, is provided by the legal theory to protect the individual against the state'. Thus, Islamic law is 'fundamentally opposed to the notion of an independent judiciary fearlessly defining the limits of the

power of the State over the individual and powerful enough to give effect to its decisions'. The judge (*qadi*) is merely the 'legal secretary' of the caliph or political authority, who has executive discretion, according to Coulson, to extort confessions by torture, individually determine the scope of crimes and punishments, and grant extralegal jurisdiction to police agents. Others such as Abdul Aziz-Said agree that 'Islamic legal theory provides no adequate machinery to safeguard individual rights against the state'.[29]

(iv)   The *umma* and *dar al-Islam*

The word *umma*, meaning 'people', 'community' or 'nation', is the word that is used most frequently to describe the community of Muslims all over the world. *Dar al-Islam*, the house, abode or realm of Islam, is those parts of the world in which Islam rules. Everything outside is therefore *dar al-harb*, the house of war, and Muslims have an obligation to engage in *jihad* in order to extend the area over which Islam rules. At times *jihad* has been thought of as purely defensive, but at others offensive. There has been considerable discussion as to whether it means 'actual military conflict, or only political, religious, and psychological propagandizing, with perpetual readiness for war'.[30] One Muslim jurist, al-Shaybani (AD 749–805) spoke of the Muslim world as one nation forming a single state, whose goal was to conquer non-Muslim nations.[31] In the sixteenth century the lawyers felt the need to soften the harshness of the distinction between the two realms, and began to speak of an area in between the two realms, *dar al-sulh*, *dar al-ahd*, or *dar al-mu'ahada*, the realm of peace or covenant, in which Muslims were ruled by non-Muslims but allowed to practise their religion. In recent years Muslims have given a more inward and spiritual interpretation of *jihad*, seeing it as the struggle within every individual against wrong desires.[32]

(v)   *dhimmis*

Jews and Christians were recognized from the time of the Prophet as 'People of the Book' and therefore given a special status as protected people (*dhimmis*). They had to pay a special tax (*jizya*, Q. 9:29), and were exempt from military duty (see Chapter 1).

(vi) The process of formulating *shari'a* law

Shari'a is based on two main sources: the Qur'an and the Sunna (the corpus of literature known as *hadith* that records the sayings and actions of the Prophet). So, for example, in formulating laws relating to non-Muslims in Muslim countries, the lawyers would appeal to verses like: 'There is no compulsion in religion' (2:256). In order to interpret the verse, they would describe different situations in the life of the Prophet in which these words may have been revealed. Thus one incident is reported in which a Muslim in Mecca wanted to know what to do with his two sons who had become Christians and wanted to go to Syria with the Christian merchants who had persuaded them. The words of the Qur'anic verse were revealed to give Muhammad the answer that he needed. Similarly, after the death of Muhammad, when the order was given for Christian and Jewish tribes in Arabia which refused to accept Islam to be driven out, the policy was based on a reported saying of the Prophet: 'two religions cannot remain together in the peninsula of the Arabs'.[33]

Two techniques or principles were used in interpreting the Qur'an and the Sunna sources. The principle of *ijma'*, consensus, encouraged the scholars to ask: what was the consensus of the companions of the Prophet and the Muslim community after his time? The principle of *qiyas*, analogy, was used in cases where there was no clear basis for a ruling in either the Qur'an or the Sunna. Here the question would be: is there a saying or action in the life of the Prophet or his companions that provides an analogy on which a ruling can be based?

The study of *shari'a*, the science of jurisprudence, is known as *fiqh*. It is important to recognize that there were four main schools of jurisprudence, and that they were not always unanimous in their interpretation of *shari'a*. 'There are remarkable differences, profound conflicts,' says Hjarpe, 'in the interpretations of the participants in the debates as to what in reality is meant by "Islamic laws".'[34] The process of legal reasoning and argument which led to the formulation of law is known as *ijtihad*, meaning literally 'endeavour'. By around AD 900 it was felt that a kind of consensus had been reached, and that there was therefore little or no room left for further discussion about the requirements of the law. This was expressed by saying that 'the door of *ijtihad*' had closed. We shall see later that in the nineteenth and twentieth centuries some Muslims began to argue for the need to reopen questions that had been regarded for centuries as closed.

3. Tensions and conflicts between United Nations and Islamic statements

The various strands of international law dealing with civil and political rights are summed up in the International Bill of Human Rights, which consists of the Universal Declaration of Human Rights (1948), the International Covenant on Economics, Social and Cultural Rights (1966),[35] and the International Covenant on Civil and Political Rights (1966). The majority of these individual covenants have been adopted by all Muslim countries. Mayer argues therefore that 'since Muslim countries have, without exception, joined the international community of nations formed under United Nations (UN) auspices, they have agreed to be bound by international law.'[36] Many Muslims believe that there is no conflict between Islam and an acceptance of human rights norms, and condemn violations of human rights in Muslim countries.[37] In recent years, however, some groups of Muslims have attempted to write their own statements of universal human rights. Two of these have received wide recognition among Muslims.

The *Universal Islamic Declaration of Human Rights* (1981), produced by the Islamic Council of Europe, is a conservative document with apologetic intentions. A Muslim writer, Ali Merad, describes it as 'an important step towards reconciling Islamic tradition with the modern demand for freedom'.[38] An article produced by the German churches gives a similar evaluation: 'This document, ambivalent as it is, may be read as a cautious attempt to bring *shari'a* closer to the concept of human rights without breaking with tradition.'[39]

The *Declaration of Human Rights in Islam* (1990) came out of a convention of the Organisation of the Islamic Conference (OIC), held in Cairo, and represented an attempt 'to embody a more general consensus – although only at government level – of how Islam should affect human rights'.[40] Many Western commentators find it disappointing and see it as a step backwards, believing that it fails to focus on the main conflicts, remains ambiguous, and tends to harmonize contradictions. One writer suggests that it represents 'an orientation crisis, though not yet admitted openly'.[41] In both these documents there are often significant differences between the official text, which is in Arabic, and the English translation.

When these Islamic statements are compared with the UN Declaration and the various covenants based on it, the following areas of tension or conflict become apparent.

(i)   Assumptions about the concept of human rights

In contrast to Islamic statements which stress human obligations based on the revealed law of the Creator God, the concept of human rights in the UN documents is based on the following assumptions:

(a)   Religion is a matter of *personal, individual choice*. Secularism is implied in expressions like 'human sovereignty' and the idea that the 'will of the people shall be the basis of the authority of government'.
(b)   Human rights have *universal claim*, because they are normative demands for *all*.
(c)   All people have a right to *freedom, equality* and *fraternity*.
(d)   The law is not regarded as divine law in any sense, and human rights need to be *guaranteed and implemented by the legislation of individual states*.

(ii)   The ruling out of distinctions

UN Article 2 states that equality is to be 'without distinctions of any kind . . .' Islamic law, however, takes distinctions for granted. Muslim writers have acknowledged the tension at this point. Charfi speaks of the 'three great inequalities' in the Islamic legal tradition: between men and women; between Muslims and non-Muslims; and between freemen and slaves.[42] Abdullah' Ahmed An-Na'im writes: 'The principles of non-discrimination on grounds of gender, religion, or belief is fundamental to all the international obligations that Muslim states have undertaken under these instruments.'[43] At the same time he recognizes that: '*Shari'a* does not conceive of women and non-Muslims as full citizens of an Islamic state . . . *Shari'a* is inconsistent with the fundamental constitutional and human rights of non-Muslim citizens of an Islamic state.'[44]

(iii) Women

UN Article 16.1 speaks of 'equal rights as to marriage, during marriage and its dissolution'. In Islamic law, however, a Muslim woman cannot marry a non-Muslim man; and the right of divorce is given to women on certain conditions only. The treatment of women, who are considered as the wards of men, has been described as 'probably the most celebrated inequality under traditional Islamic law'.[45] Mayer summarizes the traditional Islamic views about the status of women as reflected in the Islamic documents on human rights:

> In these various approaches to women's rights there is an absence of any willingness to recognize women as full, equal human beings who deserve the same rights and freedoms as men. Instead, discrimination against women is treated as something entirely natural – in much the same way that people in the West think it is natural that mentally defective persons and young children must be denied certain rights and freedoms. However, there is a general reluctance to spell out in ways likely to come to the attention of a Western audience the authors' beliefs in inherent female inferiority.[46]

(iv) Freedom of thought, conscience and religion

UN Article 18 gives every individual the right to 'freedom to change his religion or belief'. In Islam, however, freedom of expression and religious freedom are defined within the *dhimma* system. Majid Khadduri recognizes that 'Individual freedom in Islam is perhaps the most difficult to relate to the modern concept of freedom.'[47] The conservative Iranian scholar, Sultanhussein Tabandeh, states frankly his belief that 'Islam never allows a Muslim to come under the authority of a non-Muslim in any circumstance at all.'[48]

(v) Punishment

UN Article 5 says: 'No one shall be subjected to torture or to cruel, inhuman or degrading treatment or punishment.' Islamic *hudud* punishments, however, include stoning, lashing and mutilation; and *qisas*, the law of retaliation, is accepted.

(vi) *Jihad*

'Conducting holy war,' says Mayer, 'is obviously incompatible with the modern scheme of relations between nation-states.'[49] Arzt explains the tensions at this point:

> The doctrine of *jihad* and the two 'abodes', war and Islam – to which the vast majority of orthodox Muslim scholars still subscribe, at least in theory – are clearly incompatible with the fundamental premise of modern international law: peaceful co-existence between coequal states. Moreover the traditional notion that treaties are limited in duration raises the question whether Islamic states intend to comply permanently with international agreements meant to be permanent.[50]

In noting these tensions between Western and Islamic approaches to human rights, however, we should not automatically conclude that they result from fundamental conflicts between 'Islam' and 'the West'. Indeed Mayer believes that the approach to human rights in the Islamic human-rights statements is to be explained more in terms of negative reactions to the West and the political self-interest of groups in positions of power than in terms of the basic theological instincts of Islam:

> These Islamic human rights schemes are products of the political context in which they emerged. Their Islamic pedigrees are dubious, and the principles they contain do not represent the outcome of rigorous, scholarly analyses of the Islamic sources or a coherent approach to Islamic jurisprudence. Instead, they seem largely shaped by their conservative authors' negative reactions to the model of freedom in Western societies and the scope of rights protections afforded by the International Bill of Human Rights.

> In producing their Islamic human rights schemes, the authors used material from the Islamic heritage, often confused with the values found in traditional societies, in a highly selective manner, resulting in a one-sided representation of Islamic teachings relating to rights that suited the authors' conservative proclivities. Anti-Western attitudes and cultural nationalism have also influenced the way the authors perceive the Islamic tradition. They have been disinclined to seek a synthesis of Islamic and international human rights norms that could serve the cause of curbing the actual patterns of human rights violations. All this leads to the conclusion that the pattern of diluted rights in the Islamic human rights schemes examined here should not be ascribed to peculiar features of Islam or its inherent incompatibility with human rights. Instead, these diluted rights should be seen as part of a broader phenomenon of attempts by elites – the beneficiaries of undemocratic and hierarchical systems – to legitimize their opposition to human rights by appealing to supposedly distinctive cultural traditions.[51]

4. Fundamental issues

It is hardly appropriate for outside observers to make moral judgments or to suggest to Muslims how they should deal with these tensions. What we can do, however, is to attempt to

highlight some of the crucial questions which need to be faced,
and to recognize that not all Muslims give the same answers
to these questions.

(i) Can Islamic law be reformed?

The fundamental issue is whether it is permissible for Muslims
to reopen questions that have been regarded as closed for a
thousand years. Are Muslims allowed to open the door of *ijtihad*,
to go back to the original sources (Qur'an and Sunna) and thus
by a process of 'independent juristic reasoning'[52] arrive at new
formulations of *shari'a* law appropriate for a particular society
today? The conservatives tend to say 'no', while others say 'yes',
insisting that 'it must remain open to every Muslim to offer her
or his views and interpretation . . .'[53] Hjarpe sums up the very
real dilemma of Muslims at this point:

> Here we find the fundamental conflict in the internal debate on
> the Muslim world: Who, which authority, which instance is it that
> ultimately decides what the will of God is? Who, which power or
> institution, is the actual expression of God's sovereignty? Is it the
> will of the people as expressed in parliament . . . or is it the spe-
> cialists, 'those with competence', the *fuquha*, 'the jurisprudents'?[54]

We have already noted the process by which *shari'a* was
formulated and became virtually fixed by around AD 900.
During the nineteenth and early twentieth centuries, however, the laws of a number of countries developed considerably under colonial rule, incorporating elements from British
and French law. Norman Anderson has described as follows
the process by which Muslim jurists attempted to change and
adapt premodern Islamic law during this period:

(a) They adopted a procedural device which left the law itself
    unchanged, but required that certain parts of it should be
    enforced only in specific circumstances.
(b) They constructed laws thought to be necessary for the
    present time, basing them on a selection of legal opinions
    of well-known jurists from the past.

(c) They claimed the right to reopen 'the door of *ijtihad*', thus putting the *shari'a* on one side and attempting to reinterpret the original sources of the law in a completely new way.

(d) They introduced legislation based on any of the previous three methods, sometimes with the assertion that it was 'not contrary to Islamic law'.[55]

The existence of such well-established precedents for adapting Islamic law explains why Arzt can argue that 'the process of formulating a modern *shari'a* of human rights from a number of sources has begun'.[56] A number of Muslims, however, are not so optimistic that it is possible to adapt Islamic law in this way. An-Na'im explains the fundamental problem in these terms:

> In addition to this most serious obstacle facing freedom of thought and expression under *shari'a*, there remains the problem of the limitations of *ijtihad* itself. According to both its textual authority and original logic, orthodox *ijtihad* cannot be exercised in matters governed by clear and definite texts of the Qur'an or *sunna*. According to historical Islamic jurisprudence, jurists may have some room for interpretation within the limits of a clear and definite text of the Qur'an and/or *sunna*, but they may not exercise *ijtihad* to develop alternative rules in any matter on which clear and definite texts can be found. Thus, any rule of *shari'a* that is based on clear and definite texts of the Qur'an and/or *sunna*, as is the case with some of the rules discriminating against women and non-Muslims, cannot be changed or modified through the use of orthodox *ijtihad*.[57]

This dilemma is particularly acute over the status of women and the status of non-Muslims.[58]

(ii) Can the concept of *dhimma* be changed or put aside?

The question here is whether Muslims want to hold on to the concept of *dhimma* in the pluralist world of today. Some of the more conservative believe that the concept is so fundamental to Islam that it cannot be surrendered. Muhammad

Hamidullah, for example, believes that 'the question of "dhimmis" cannot be resolved. Islam has chosen identity of religion as the basis of its nationality, while others think in terms of colour, language, birth-place and the like.'[59]

The view of a number of scholars, however, is that there is no place for the *dhimma* system today. Shams Iddin, for example, the acting head of Shi'ite Community in Lebanon, has stated publicly his belief that it is no longer appropriate.[60] Mohamed Talbi is equally outspoken:

> Today we live in a world where *dhimmis* no longer should exist. It has become imperative and absolutely indispensable to shelve this notion in the cupboard of history, something which from the point of view of Islam I deem absolutely possible. We face here an evolution which, according to my point of view, is part and parcel of the very meaning of Islam, of an Islam which today subscribes – with certain reserves – to human rights.[61]

Similarly, Walid Saif argues for 'total equality of Muslim and Christian citizens in an Islamic state', believing that the *dhimma* status should be discarded. He thinks that far from expressing a minority view, his position represents a consensus among Muslim scholars today.[62]

(iii)   Can the Law of Apostasy be reinterpreted?

If we ask whether the requirement of premodern *shari'a* should be retained in a modern state, Abul ala Mawdudi stands uncompromisingly by the traditional view:

> To everyone acquainted with Islamic law it is no secret that according to Islam the punishment for a Muslim who turns to *kufr* (infidelity, blasphemy) is execution. Doubt about this matter first arose among Muslims during the final portion of the nineteenth century as a result of speculation. Otherwise, for the full twelve centuries prior to that time the total Muslim community remained unanimous about it . . . All these collectively will assure you that from the time of the Prophet to the present day one injunction only has been continuously and uninterruptedly operative and

that no room whatever remains to suggest that perhaps the punishment of the apostate is not execution.[63]

Muhammad Hamidullah holds the same view, but is aware of some of the difficulties:

> The question of apostasy is also difficult to resolve. Islam demands for itself the liberty of preaching, but does not give liberty to a Muslim to abandon his religion. Theoretically, it is a weak point for Islam to defend, but in practice it has no importance, except in extremely rare cases. For not only in countries under Muslim rule, even in a non-Muslim environment cases of Muslims abandoning their religion are practically non-existent. Christian colonial rule proved this premise.[64]

It would seem that this traditional view is maintained in all of the Islamic statements on human rights already noted, since none of them takes a position on the question of apostasy. Mayer concludes: 'The authors' unwillingness to repudiate the rule that a person should be executed over a question of religious beliefs reveals the enormous gap that exists between their mentalities and the modern philosophy of human rights ... the authors have neglected to confront and resolve the main issues involved in harmonizing international human rights and *shari'a* standards.'[65]

Alongside this traditional view, however, there are individuals like Fazlur Rahman who have argued that the death penalty for apostasy cannot be based on the Qur'an: 'If apostasy had been considered a punishable crime in this world, the Qur'an would certainly have provided some punishment. But the Qur'an only says that upon such people, i.e. those who repeatedly apostasized, there shall be God's curse. This shows that the mediaeval law of apostasy of Islam is out of agreement with the Qur'an.'[66] Since there is a clear difference of opinion among Muslims on this issue, with a large number of Muslims who are convinced that traditional rules about apostasy no longer apply, we need to recognize that in many situations today factors *other than Islam* are at work. Mayer believes that certain individuals and governments choose not to allow this development of Islamic law for reasons which have little to do with Islam:

> Muslims who currently call for the execution of apostates are not compelled to do so by unambiguous Islamic authority supporting the death penalty. There is diversity of opinion and ample ground for deciding that the premodern *shari'a* rules on apostasy no longer apply. Muslims can select alternative interpretations of the Islamic rules on apostasy that are more in keeping with the tenor of the Qur'an and with modern human rights norms on religious freedom. Where they elect not to do so and insist that apostates should be executed, one must wonder whether they are in reality motivated by opposition to the principle of religious freedom and are constructing Islamic rationales to legitimize that opposition.[67]

(iv) How valid is the appeal to cultural relativity?

Should Muslims be able to claim that while they subscribe to internationally recognized statements on human rights, they must have the freedom to be flexible and to apply these principles in a way that is appropriate in the light of a country's history and culture? Some Muslims like Cherif Bassiouni believe that they must have this freedom: 'Nothing in Islamic international law precludes the applicability of these international obligations to the domestic legal system of an Islamic state *provided these obligations are not contrary to Shari'ah* . . . [international human rights] are subject to the purposes and objectives of a given society, subject to the due process of law.'[68]

Others, however, reject this view, pointing out that allowing this reservation would 'render a basic international obligation of a contractual nature meaningless'. It would 'undermine the basis of international contractual law'.[69] An-Na'im similarly points out the implications of accepting the principle of cultural relativity:

> The Muslims are not to be allowed to treat religious minorities in this way because they believe that their own religious law authorizes them to do so. Otherwise, we would have to accept not only similar mistreatment of Muslim minorities in non-Islamic states,

but also that complete negation of all the achievements of the domestic civil liberties and international human rights violations, including torture and even genocide, may be rationalized or justified with reference to alleged religious and cultural codes or norms.[70]

Mayer believes that it is becoming harder and harder for Muslim governments to justify deviations from international law by appealing to Islam and the principle of cultural relativity:

> As of 1994, there is evidence that even the countries that were most adamant about the need to apply Islamic law are developing ambivalence about the degree to which appeals to Islam can justify their deviations from international law. Although official support for the proposition that Islam mandates a distinctive approach to human rights could be said to have grown in the 1990s with the issuance of the Cairo Declaration and the Saudi Basic Law, other indications are that Muslim states are beginning to come to terms with the high degree of authority and normative force that international human rights have won. Despite governmental attempts to crush independent Muslim human rights advocacy, the impact of human rights ideals is proving so potent that governments are increasingly trying to co-opt human rights, offering concessions, albeit only cosmetic ones, to demands that they show respect for rights. Islamic legitimacy is, it seems, becoming difficult to sustain in the absence of a legitimacy that is grounded in respect for human rights.[71]

(v) What factors are at work other than Islam?

It needs to be recognized that in many countries Islam may not be the only factor or even the main factor in debates about human rights. 'I see Islam as only one factor in the reception of human rights in the Middle East,' says Ann Elizabeth Mayer. 'My experience in work on behalf of the cause of human rights would have sufficed to convince me that Islam is not the cause of the human rights problems endemic to the Middle East.'[72] Governments, for example, are not only concerned about Muslims leaving Islam for religious reasons, but are aware of a variety of other reasons for which they might want to leave Islam. Some women could try to renounce Islam in order to evade *shari'a* legislation over marriage or other questions concerning personal status, or to obtain divorce more easily. The conservative Iranian scholar, Tabandeh, believes that 'the temptation to escape a marriage by apostasy is a real threat and . . . a strong deterrent is necessary to prevent women from using apostasy in this way.'[73] Saif notes other factors affecting human rights which have nothing to do with Islam: 'The role of dictatorship, state oppression, lack of institutional democracy, absence of social justice, the failure of alien models of development insensitive to local culture, and Western domination'.

In many other situations governments appeal to the Law of Apostasy simply in order to suppress a minority view. Perhaps the clearest example of this response was the execution of Mahmud Muhammad Taha by the Sudanese government in February 1985 which was carried out largely because of his political opposition to Nimeiri's regime and his criticism of the policies of 'Islamization'. In cases like these, what is happening, in Mayer's words, is that 'Policies serve the interests of powerful groups already enjoying privileged positions.'[74] She concludes:

> The possibility must be borne in mind that Islamization is becoming associated with practices and policies shaped by political forces – quite separate from Islam as a religion – reflecting the mundane political interests of groups that have much to lose by the advance of freedom and democracy in the Muslim world. A skeptic could propose that official Islamization policies are no more than a strategy adopted by beleaguered elites in an attempt to trump growing Muslim demands for democratization and human rights. These elites may be making cynical appeals to divine authority as the rationale for oppressive, exploitative rule and a regime of inequality and discrimination.[75]

(vi) How do we accept the gulf between the ideal and the actual?

It is some encouragement in this debate that both Muslims and Christians recognize the ambiguities and the discrepancies between the ideal and the real:

It is a well-known phenomenon in human religious history that the high moral and spiritual ideals of religious traditions remain a challenge for the faith-communities concerned which have often either flagrantly violated these ideals, or seriously undermined them (Mahmoud Ayoub).[76]

What is often seen by its neighbours, and by some Muslims themselves, as 'Islamic' may in fact be the product of cultural attitudes and móres or local history. For this reason, a purely theoretical study of the basic teachings of Islam concerning non-Muslim minorities would be insufficient if it did not take into consideration the diverse local situations in which Islamic teaching is actually lived by Muslims. Although this perception may be challenged by Muslim scholars, the fact remains that, for the non-Muslim, 'Islam' is not only what is taught in the Qur'an and Sunna but also what is seen to be professed and practised by the community of Muslims. What the non-Muslim sees often differs from one geographical region and cultural situation to the next. Thus, the theoretical or dogmatic study of what is taught by the sources of Islamic faith must be balanced by how this teaching is applied and modified in concrete situations in life (Thomas Michel).[77]

In spite of this, however, non-Muslims often find it hard to reconcile the eirenic statements of Muslim scholars with what actually happens in practice in many countries, with government support or encouragement, when Muslims change their religion. While many in the West may welcome the more liberal statements by Muslims of the ideals of Islam, they cannot help wondering how many decades or centuries it will be before the passion and wounded pride of a family threatened with the loss of one of its members (which have little to do with Islam) will be controlled more effectively by governments and Muslim leaders. The more often people in the West hear conservative Muslims reaffirming a very traditional view of the punishment to be meted out to an apostate, the more they will suspect that the death penalty for apostasy may after all be the most consistent Islamic response to those who choose to leave the fold of Islam, simply because it seems to be most in keeping with classical sources and is still such a common response today.

5. The call for the reform of Islamic law

In order to challenge the stereotype of Islam as a religion that is monolithic and unable to change, it is important to recognize the wide variety of views among Muslims on the subject of human rights. At the risk of over-simplification, it may be possible to identify at least five different positions among Muslim scholars and leaders:

(a) *A conservative view*, common among traditional religious scholars, which upholds a very long-established inter-pretations of Islamic law, insisting, for example, on the application of the laws of punishment.
(b) *'A fundamentalist' view*, which, while urging a return to tradi-tional values, stresses the importance of re-interpreting the law and shows a degree of flexibility in principle.
(c) *A modernist view*, which recognizes that while the *spirit* of *shari'a* is eternal, the *letter* is not, and needs to be adapted in changing circumstances.
(d) *'A wide middle ground'*, which argues for a more pragmatic approach, and which finds ways of reconciling Islamic law with modern legal standards.
(e) *A more liberal or radical view*, which believes that certain aspects of traditional Islamic law can and must be com-pletely revised or even set aside in the light of fundamental Islamic values.

If there is this kind of diversity in the views of Muslim scholars, and if some in particular are calling for new approaches to human rights issues, how do they argue their case? The follow-ing three writers are examples of Muslims who regard them-selves as fully within the Islamic tradition, but who plead very openly for the reform of Islamic law. They come originally from Lebanon, Tunisia and Sudan. In each case we find that while they accept recent developments in Western thinking and are therefore critical of conservative Muslim approaches, they believe that they can undergird their acceptance of new ideas by appeal to thoroughly Islamic principles based on the Qur'an and the earliest traditions. It is worth persevering with some of the technical arguments they use, because of the light they shed on the way Muslims think about questions to do with Islamic law.

(i) Mahmoud Ayoub (b. 1935)

Ayoub is a Lebanese Shi'ite Muslim, who is now professor of Islamic Studies at the Department of Religion, Temple University. In an article entitled 'Religious Freedom and the Law of Apostasy in Islam', he begins by explaining that later Muslim jurists defined *ridda* (apostasy) 'so broadly as to include any statement, action or belief that may contradict Islam or defame any of its sacred books or personages'.[78] He says that the Qur'an 'categorically repudiates religious coercion and affirms that faith and rejection of faith, right guidance and misguidance ultimately rest with God to give or withhold as He will' (Q. 10:99; 18:29). Apostasy therefore 'ultimately lies outside the authority of the sacred law'. He then gives examples from what he calls the 'long and controversial exegetical history' of the Qur'anic verse 'there is no compulsion in religion' (2:256).

One of the 'occasions of revelation' given by commentators to explain the circumstances in which the words were revealed describes an incident concerning a man of Medina whose two sons converted to Christianity under the influence of Syrian oil merchants. 'The two youths decided to migrate to Syria with their Christian mentors. Angry and disappointed, their father went to the Prophet and asked if he should pursue them and forcefully bring them back. The verse was revealed, and the Prophet said: "May God remove them far away; they are the first people to reject faith".'

One commentator appealed to the principle of abrogation, arguing that the prohibition of coercion is abrogated by a later verse in which the Muslims are commanded to fight against those who do not believe (Q. 9:29). Ayoub explains:

> The absolute imperative of religious freedom just discussed is blatantly contradicted in another exegetical opinion attributed to the famous companion and *hadith* transmitter Abu Hurayrah. The

Qur'an challenges the Muslims to be 'the best community brought forth for humankind' through enjoining the good, dissuading from evil and having true faith in God (Q. 2:10). Abu Hurayrah commented on the verse, saying, 'You are the best people for humankind as you bring them in chains into Islam'.[79]

Two stories related in *hadith* were frequently used as a basis for the Law of Apostasy, although they actually reveal 'the persistent division of later jurists on this issue'. Ayoub concludes:

> The two traditions . . . clearly contradict one another. This, and the fact that neither appears to have a credible historical or legal context, lead one to believe that Mu'adh's account has been used to argue for a summary execution of apostates, while that of 'Umar is meant to support the more widely held view that an apostate should be given a three-day respite to repent. Although a general consensus has emerged on the side of giving the apostate an opportunity to repent, the practice appears to have begun as a moral expedient based on the Qur'anic principles of human repentance and divine forgiveness, rather than a specific *hadith* legislation.[80]

Ayoub then discusses two sayings of the Prophet that clearly stipulate the death penalty for apostasy. Firstly, 'he who changes his religion, kill him'. Ayoub believes that the apostates here were not Jews or Christians, and that the *hadith* is too vague to serve as a basis for law. One of the sayings reported in the incident he believes to be 'a legal fiction, but with an extraneous political aim'. Secondly, the saying that 'he who abandons his religion' should be killed, is, he believes, of late origin, and since it was probably directed against the Kharijites, it represents 'a repudiation of extremism and disunity' rather than legislation for apostasy. Ayoub therefore believes that 'there is no real basis for the *riddah* law in either the Qur'an or Prophetic tradition'.

His final conclusion draws attention to the way in which the political context has frequently contributed to the hardening of attitudes and traditions concerning apostasy:

A careful study of the early sources of Islamic tradition reveals an increasingly hardening attitude towards apostasy. This attitude is reflected in the harsh laws which grew harsher as the political, economic and religious interrelations among the three communities of the book worsened.

While the legal judgments may be harsh and uncompromising, they remain somewhat tentative and widely divergent . . . the principle in all this is not to find a way to punish a would be apostate, but rather to find a way out for him or her . . . Apostasy was never a problem for the Muslim community. It remained a theoretical issue because the people executed for apostasy until the end of the 'Abbasid caliphate in the thirteenth century were very few. Apostasy became a political issue with the rise of Western colonialism and consequent intensification of Western Christian missionary activities in Muslim areas.[81]

(ii) Mohamed Talbi (b. 1921)

The Tunisian historian Mohamed Talbi is significant because of the way he challenges an excessively legalistic under-standing of *shari'a*, and highlights the ethical core of the Qur'an. In an article entitled 'Religious Liberty: A Muslim perspective' he begins by acknowledging that 'religious liberty is today, as a matter of fact, definitely and for good rooted in our social life. Since the *Declaration of Human Rights* in 1948, this concept is henceforth an essential part of international law . . . we already live in a pluralist world, and our world is going to be more and more pluralist in the near future . . . there is no longer any room for exclusiveness.'[82] He points out that the Muslim world has only recently begun to be confronted with secularism. 'It is now our turn to experience from the inside the growth of agnosticism and atheism.'

Talbi defines religious liberty as

Basically the right to decide for oneself, without any kind of pressure, fear or anxiety, the right to believe or not to believe, the right to assume with full consciousness one's destiny, the right of course to get rid of all kinds of faith as superstition inherited from the dark ages, but the right also to espouse the faith of one's choice, to worship and to bear witness freely.[83]

He believes that this concept of religious liberty is in harmony with the Qur'an because it is 'basically founded . . . first and foremost on the divinely ordered nature of man . . . So from a Qur'anic perspective we may say that human rights are rooted in what every man is by nature . . . Now it goes without saying that the corner stone of all human rights is religious liberty.'[84]

It is vital, therefore, that every person should be able 'to choose his way freely and without any kind of coercion . . . faith, to be true and reliable faith, needs absolutely to be a free and voluntary act'. Man 'has the capacity to resist God's call, and this capacity is the criterion of his true freedom . . . God has set man truly and tragically free.'[85] Elsewhere he explains more fully the theological basis of his insistence on human freedom and religious liberty:

> From a Muslim perspective and based on the Koranic teachings . . . religious liberty is an act of fundamental respect for the sovereignty of God and the secret of his intentions towards man who has been endowed with the frightening privilege of taking over his destiny on earth and in the hereafter, in personal responsibility. Respecting human freedom ultimately means respecting God's intention. Being a true Muslim means subjecting oneself to the will of God. It means putting one's existence in the hands of God – willingly, and full of trust and love.[86]

Religious liberty, however, does not mean 'an attitude of abandon and indifference'. Man's fulfilment as a creature is 'in his reconciliation at once to God and to people'. The challenge therefore is to find 'the way . . . to bring about this double reconciliation, without betraying God and without damaging the inner life and the other person'.[87] So 'to be a true Muslim is to live in a courteous dialogue with all peoples of other faiths and ideologies and ultimately to submit to God.' Therefore 'our duty is just to bear witness and in the most courteous way, the one most respectful of the inner liberty of our neighbour and of his sacredness.'

Talbi then argues that Muslims today need to find ways of going 'beyond the limits imposed by the traditional theology' because this traditional theology 'developed in a way that . . . does not always fit in with the spirit of the Qur'an'. He tackles the two key questions of *dhimmi* status and apostasy. He believes that in practice 'Islam itself was never imposed by compulsion', and that at its best this system actually improved the condition of Christians and Jews. He recognizes, however, that they did at times suffer from discrimination, especially under al-Mutawakkil (AD 847–61) and al-Hakim (AD 996–1021). 'In the mediaeval context of wars, hostilities and treacheries, this policy of discrimination or open oppression was always prompted, or strongly backed, by the theologians.' We must remember, however, that 'it was not then a virtue to consider all human beings as equal. How to consider equal Truth and Error, true believers and heretics!?'

In discussing apostasy he believes that here again 'traditional theology did not remain faithful to the spirit of the Qur'an'. He recognizes that this theology makes it 'practically impossible, once inside Islam, to leave it', but does not know of any instances when the law condemning apostates to death was applied. He suggests different ways of interpreting the various *hadith*: for example: in some the major crime referred to is not apostasy but rebellion and/or highway robbery; another *hadith* is not binding and was 'undoubtedly forged'. The Law of Apostasy is at variance with the Qur'an, where there is no mention of the death penalty. 'The punishment of the apostate . . . is left to God's judgment and to the after-life . . . The Qur'an strives to raise the new Muslims' spirit in order to prevent them from falling into apostasy.[88] The debate is between God and the apostate's conscience and it is not our role to interfere in it.' It also warns that there is 'no hope for those who persist in their apostasy'. He finally concludes that 'the Qur'an argues, warns, advises, but never resorts to the argument of the sword. The reason why is that argument is meaningless in matters of faith. In our pluralistic world our modern theologians must take that into account.'[89]

Talbi is therefore an example of a Muslim scholar who accepts much of Western thinking about religious liberty, and argues strongly for the reform of Islamic law in certain areas by appealing to basic Islamic principles which he finds in the Qur'an and the earliest Islamic traditions.

(iii)   Abdallah Ahmed An-Na'im

An-Na'im is a Sudanese Muslim who taught for some years in the Faculty of Law at Khartoum University before going to the USA. He now teaches at Emory School of Law in the USA. In Mayer's view he is particularly important because he has worked out a clear methodology for approaching questions of Islamic law today: 'Offering a methodology that allows a fresh approach to the Islamic sources, An-Na'im has been able to develop a coherent scheme of human rights principles that is, for those who accept the validity of the proposed methodology, also one that emanates from Islamic values and principles.'[90]

His starting point is that while the Qur'an and the Sunna should be regarded by Muslims as 'perfect and infallible', the *shari'a* should not. He believes that the techniques for law reform developed by early Muslim jurists are 'inadequate and incapable of solving the problems or supplementing the deficiencies'.[91] What he goes on to offer, therefore, is 'a comprehensive theory for modern Islamization',[92] based on the teaching of Mahmud Muhammad Taha, a Sudanese Muslim scholar who established the Republican Party in 1945 and was executed publicly by President Nimeiri's government in February 1985 on a charge of heresy and sedition. It is widely believed that the public revulsion within the country over the execution of an 80 year old man was a major factor contributing to Nimeiri's downfall.[93] Taha's desire to find a completely new approach to Islamic legislation developed out of a profound spiritual experience after his release from prison in 1948 and during three years of seclusion following the Sufi tradition.

In summarizing Taha's approach, An-Na'im advocates what is known as 'abrogation in reverse', the principle that instead of believing that the *later* revelation always abrogates an *earlier* revelation, in some cases the *earlier* can abrogate the *later*:

This technique is based on the fundamental proposition that both the Qur'an and the *sunna* should be seen as containing two messages; the primary and permanent message of the Mecca stage, and the subsidiary and traditional message of the Medina stage. Both messages were revealed in the Qur'an to the Prophet Muhammad, who is the final Prophet in accord with Muslim belief. In view of persistent and violent rejection by the Meccans of the fundamental principles of justice and equality contained in the Mecca message, Islam implemented, as its First Message, the principles of relative justice and equality, which were more appropriate to the concrete circumstances of the seventh century. Now that humanity has achieved sufficient advances through human endeavour as guided by God, including the application of the First Message, it is now appropriate . . . to implement the primary and permanent message, which would be, in chronological order of implementation, the Second Message of Islam. According to this logic, certain aspects of the Qur'an and *sunna* revealed and uttered during the subsequent stage of Medina should be seen as of transitional, *not* permanent application. When it is appropriate to do so, the transitional aspects of *sharia* should be replaced by the fundamental principles of the Qur'an and *sunna* of the earlier Mecca period. In other words, Islamic legislation should be elevated from one level of the Qur'an and *sunna* to another higher level of the same Qur'an and *sunna*.[94]

As an example of this approach, Taha taught that while the Qur'an and *sunna* during the Medina period taught discrimination against women and non-Muslims, during the Meccan period they 'provided for complete equality and freedom for both women and non-Muslims'.[95] Thus 'the texts of Mecca do provide for fundamental principles of justice and equality, while those of Medina permit discrimination on grounds of gender and religion.'[96]

Conclusion

(a) If Christians continue to protest about the treatment of converts, as they undoubtedly will do, they must be prepared to see the question of apostasy in its broader context. When some Christian organizations focus only on the persecution of Christians and the burning of churches in Muslim countries, there is a danger that they are creating an unrepresentative picture of the Muslim world and simply feeding the fears and stereotypes of Western Christians. When Christians protest, they must be seen to be protesting also about wider issues concerning human rights. And they should be just as vocal in their condemnation of unfair treatment of Muslim minorities in the West.

(b) People in the West must resist the oversimplification which assumes that everything that Muslims say and do concerning human rights must be related to Islam. Mayer sums up this conclusion perfectly when she says, 'I see Islam as only one factor in the reception of human rights in the Middle East . . . Islam is not the cause of the human rights problems endemic in the Middle East.' Her work is particularly valuable for the way she shows that governments guilty of human rights abuses are often using Islam for political purposes that have nothing to do with Islam. If these governments are prepared to use any means they can find to keep themselves in power, non-Muslims must resist the temptation to blame all the actions of those governments on Islam.

(c) The West must be prepared to recognize the diversity of views among Muslims. It is totally unhelpful for Westerners to suggest that all Muslims are the same and cannot change their beliefs, and to assume that the most conservative and fundamentalist interpretations of Islam necessarily represent the true spirit of the religion. If Christians believe that they themselves have the freedom to change their interpretation of the Bible or of Christian doctrine, they must allow Muslims the freedom to do the same.

(d) It is also important to recognize the seriousness of the dilemmas facing Muslims. It is no exaggeration for Mohamed Talbi to speak of 'a truly rending problem for devout Muslims'. Mayer is remarkably frank about the two options facing Muslim governments: 'The stage seems to be set for efforts to mesh Islamic law and its attendant values with human rights. Whether the result will be a fruitful and constructive combination of the two or more official hypocrisy, only time will tell.'[97]

(e) Since people in the West, including Christians, now take so much of recent thinking about human rights for granted, they are likely to have considerable sympathy for Muslims who occupy the 'wide middle ground' or who hold to a more liberal or radical view. If some will choose to believe that only the very conservative view represents the true spirit of Islam, others will want to identify themselves with Muslims who are seeking to reform Islamic law by going back to the sources and finding new ways of interpreting them. Any Christian response on these issues, however, is likely to be open to criticism from Muslims. If Christians support modernist or liberal Muslim views, they are sometimes accused of trying to 'Christianize' Islam, but if they suggest that the more conservative views are more faithful to the spirit of Islam, they can be accused of portraying Islam, as backward and incapable of reform.

(f) Christians should perhaps be willing to acknowledge more openly some of the areas of common ground with Muslims in discussion about human rights. They should, for example, be the first to agree with Muslims that one cannot speak of human rights as if they exist in a vacuum, completely independent from duties and responsibilities.

In the area of human rights, therefore, it is far too simple to think in terms of a straightforward confrontation between 'Islam' and 'the West'. If Muslims have a great deal of hard thinking to do, so do people in the West. And they will need among other things to be willing to listen to what people like Walid Saif seem to be saying to the West: 'Please don't suggest that Muslims are faced with a choice: either Islam and national cultural identity or modernity, secularism and Westernization. This presents an impossible dilemma, since it is perfectly possible for Muslims to find ways of adapting to the challenges of the modern world. Modernization need not mean Westernization. So please don't drive a wedge between Islam and human rights!'

Notes

1   Quote taken from Johannes Schwartländer and Heiner Bielefeldt, 'Christians and Muslims Facing the Challenge of Human Rights', *German Bishops' Conference Research Group on the Universal Tasks of the Church*, Bonn, Jan 1994, p. 32. The report is quoting from two Muslim writers. The full quotation is: 'Muslims experience the tension between the competing normative claims as a kind of collective schizophrenia, as Charfi drastically puts it. Talbi speaks of a truly "rending" problem for devout Muslims.'

2   A.K. Brohi, 'Islam and Human Rights' in A. Gauhar, ed., *The Challenge of Islam*, London, p. 183.

3   Abul Ala Mawdudi, 'Political Theory of Islam' in *Islam: Its meaning and message*, Khurshid Ahmad (ed.), The Islamic Foundation, Leicester, 1975, p. 159.

4   Ann Elizabeth Mayer, *Islam and Human Rights: Tradition and Politics*, Pinter, London, 1995, p. 160.

5   Donna E. Arzt, 'The Application of International Human Rights Law in Islamic States', *Human Rights Quarterly*, vol. 12, 1990, p. 227.

6   Abdullah Ahmed An-Na'im, 'Mahmud Taha and the Crisis of Islamic Law Reform: Implications for Interreligious Relations', *Journal of Ecumenical Studies*, vol. 25:1, 1988, p. 8.

7   Kevin Dwyer, *Arab Voices: The human rights debate in the middle East*, Routledge, London, 1991.

8   Heiner Bielefeldt, 'International Human Rights; Challenge and opportunity to Christians and Muslims', paper presented to the workshop on *Christian Perceptions of Islam; Muslim Perceptions of Christianity: The historical record*, Royal Institute for Inter-Faith Studies, Amman, Jordan, August 1995, p. 7 (author's italics).

9   Mohamed Talbi, 'Religious Liberty: A Muslim perspective', *Islamocristiana*, vol. 11, 1985, p. 100.

10   Bielefeldt, op. cit., p. 4.

11   Mahmoud Ayoub, 'Religious Freedom and the Law of Apostasy in Islam', *Islamocristiana*, vol. 20, 1994, p. 75.

12   Bielefeldt, op. cit., p. 10.

13   Ibid., pp. 2–3.

14   Ibid., p. 6.

15   Ibid., p. 13.

[16] Marston Speight, 'A Conference on Human Rights from the Faith Perspectives of Muslims and Christians', *Islamocristiania*, 1983, No. 9, p. 162.

[17] Ayoub, op. cit., p. 75.

[18] Mayer, op. cit., pp. 127–8.

[19] Ibid., p. 124.

[20] Brohi, op. cit., p. 192.

[21] S.M. Sayed, 'Human Rights in Islam', *Hamdard Islamicus*, vol. ix, no. 3, p. 67.

[22] Said, 'Human Rights in Islamic Perspective' in A. Pollis and P. Schwab (eds.), *Human Rights and Ideological Perspectives*, p. 92, 1980, quoted in Arzt, op. cit., p. 206.

[23] A.K. Brohi, 'The Nature of Islamic Law and the Concept of Human Rights', in International Commission of Jurists, Kuwait University and Union of Arab Lawyers, *Human Rights in Islam. Report of a seminar held in Kuwait, December, 1980.*

[24] Cherif Bassiouni, 'Sources of Islamic Law and the Protection of Human Rights in the Islamic Criminal Justice System', *The Islamic Criminal Justice System*, vol. 3, p. 23, quoted in Arzt, op. cit., p. 206. His interpolation in brackets.

[25] Mayer, op. cit., p. 38.

[26] Ibid., p. 83.

[27] Ibid.

[28] Quoted in Mayer, op. cit., p. 52.

[29] Arzt, op. cit., pp. 206–7.

[30] Ibid., p. 211.

[31] Ibid., p. 210.

[32] This interpretation of *jihad* is often based on a saying of the Prophet on returning from battle: 'We have now returned from the lesser *jihad* (i.e. fighting) to the greater *jihad*.' (See under JIHAD in Mircea Eliade, *Encyclopedia of Religion*, vol. 8, 1987, pp. 88ff.

[33] A. Guillaume, *The Life of Muhammad: A translation of Ibn Ishaq's Sirat Rasul Allah*, Oxford University Press, 1955, p. 525.

[34] Jan Hjarpe, 'Islamic Law and Discussion on Human Rights', paper presented to a *Conference on Christianity and Islam and Human Rights*, organized by the United Nations, 22–6 January 1994, p. 7; an adaptation of a study previously published in Swedish ('Islamisk ratt och diskussionen om Manskliga

rattigheter', *Retfaerd Nordisk juridisk tidsskrift*, no. 60, 1993:1, pp. 3–14.

35 Mayer, op. cit., p. 19.
36 Ibid., p. 10.
37 Ibid., p. 25.
38 Schwartländer and Bielefeldt, op. cit., p. 13.
39 Ibid., p. 34.
40 Mayer, op. cit., p. 24.
41 Schwartländer and Bielefeldt, op. cit., p. 13.
42 Ibid., p. 34.
43 An-Na'im, p. 3, footnote 3.
44 Ibid., pp. 3 and 20.
45 Arzt, op. cit., p. 8.
46 Mayer, op. cit., p. 117.
47 Arzt, op. cit., p. 5.
48 Mayer, op. cit., p. 130.
49 Ibid., p. 127.
50 Arzt, op. cit., p. 14.
51 Mayer, op. cit., p. 177.
52 An-Na'im, op. cit., p. 5.
53 Ibid., p. 8.
54 Hjarpe, op. cit., p. 6.
55 J.N.D. Anderson, *An Adopted Son: The Story of My Life*, IVP, Leicester, 1985, p. 149.
56 Arzt, op. cit., p. 28.
57 An-Na'im, op. cit., p. 9.
58 See Mayer, op. cit., pp. 79–139.
59 Muhammad Hamidullah, 'Relations of Muslims with Non-Muslims', *Journal of Muslim Minority Affairs*, vol. 7, 1936, p. 9.
60 Mehdi Shamsuddin, as reported by Tarek Mitri of the World Council of Churches. Yusuf al-Qaradawi expressed the same view in a talk show broadcast in the spring of 1997 by the satellite TV channel ART. It was also the view of Fahmy Howaridy in his book *Muwatinun La Dhimmiyun* ('Fellow-Citizens, not Dhimmis'), published by Dar al-Sharouq, Cairo, 1980.
61 Mohamed Talbi, 'Islamic-Christian Encounter Today. Some Principles', in *Christian-Muslim Encounter in the Middle East*, MECC Perspectives, no. 415, July/August, 1985, p. 10.

62 Walid Saif, 'Human Rights and Islamic Revivalism' in *Religion, Law and Society: A Christian-Muslim discussion*, Tarek Mitri (ed.), WCC, Geneva, 1995, p. 128.
63 Abul Ala Mawdudi, *The Punishment of the Apostate According to Islamic Law*, translated and annotated by Syed Silas Husain and Ernest Hahn, 1994, p. 17. Bracketed material as original.
64 Hamidullah, op. cit., p. 9.
65 Mayer, op. cit., p. 160.
66 Fazlur Rahman, 'Non-Muslim Minorities in an Islamic State', *Journal of the Institute of Muslim Minority Affairs*, vol. 7, 1986, p. 16.
67 Mayer, op. cit., p. 147.
68 Arzt, op. cit., pp. 214–15.
69 Ibid., p. 221.
70 Ibid., p. 224.
71 Mayer, op. cit., p. 183.
72 Ibid., pp. xi and xvii.
73 Ibid., p. 144.
74 Ibid., p. xv.
75 Ibid., p. 126.
76 Ayoub, op. cit., p. 78.
77 Thomas Michel, 'The Rights of Non-Muslims in Islam: An opening statement', *Journal of the Institute of Muslim Minority Affairs*, pp. 12–13.
78 Ayoub, op. cit., p. 76.
79 Ibid., p. 78.
80 Ibid., p. 82.
81 Ibid., p. 81.
82 Talbi, *Religious Liberty*, op. cit., p. 101.
83 Ibid., p. 102.
84 Ibid.
85 Ibid., p. 104.
86 Schwartländer and Bielefeldt, op. cit., pp. 30–1.
87 Talbi, *Religious Liberty*, op. cit., p. 105.
88 Ibid., pp. 109–112.
89 Ibid., p. 113.
90 Mayer, op. cit., p. 46.
91 An-Na'im, op. cit., p. 2.
92 Ibid., p. 3.

93 See Mayer, op. cit., pp. 156–9; and John L. Esposito, *The Islamic Threat: Myth or reality?*, Oxford University Press, 1992, pp. 90–1.
94 An-Naʿim, op. cit., p. 15.
95 Ibid., p. 16.
96 Ibid., p. 17.
97 Mayer, op. cit., p. 183.

Six
—

Education: From Demand to Dialogue?

Introduction

> Until Muslims can set up their own schools they should make sure that their children are carrying out their duties as Muslims in state schools (Imtiaz Karim).[1]

> Multicultural education in Britain has failed because the multiculturalists have failed to understand the nature of Islam (Mervyn Hiskett).[2]

> A pluralist society is in particular need of a culture of dialogue so that the views of all the different groupings represented can be clearly understood, and possibilities identified for shared modes of thought and conduct (Rotraud Wielandt).[3]

> Much of the dialogue carried out between Christians and Muslims today is coloured by the presence of that silent third partner: anti-religious secularism (Seyyed Hossein Nasr).[4]

In thousands of schools across Europe, Muslim children, parents, school governors and religious leaders come face to face not only with secular world-views that relegate religion to the sidelines, but also with a wide variety of expressions of Christianity and other faiths. Education is therefore an area where fundamental issues in the meeting between Islam and the West come to the surface with considerable urgency.

Our first task in this chapter is to understand the Muslim opposition to secular education and to note the requests and demands made by Muslims in the British context, recognizing the deep convictions and strong feelings that lie behind them. We then need to understand what are the main factors that determine the responses of the authorities to these requests. Questions concerning state-funded Muslim schools and collective worship are considered as test cases of the issues involved. This is followed by a discussion about Islamic approaches to pluralism, and the chapter ends with an outline of a possible basis for pluralism in British schools.

1. Islamic opposition to secular education

Within an Islamic framework the primary purpose of education, according to M.A. Bari, is 'to produce a good and righteous man who . . . tries to reach the stage of perfection as demanded by Islam'.[5] Islamic education is 'faith-motivated' and seeks to be comprehensive, in the sense that it covers every aspect of life. Because Muslims have 'fervent attachment towards their religion and culture', they feel 'so different from the majority of British people'.[6] They therefore experience 'agony' over education, 'facing a real dilemma with not only their children's education but for their overall future prospects in Britain'. They are 'genuinely fearful that their children are not immune to the overwhelming temptation and complexities of the British society'.[7] In this dilemma 'an ideal situation for them would have been a modern education for their children that conforms to the fundamentals of, or at least not contradictory to, Islamic values. But Britain is not an Islamic country and as such the Muslim idealism can not be expected to be fulfilled so easily.'

It is not surprising, therefore, that a committed Muslim educationist like Bari is so critical of the British education system, which he believes is

> based on secularism with the gloss of religion as an outsider. Its aim is to carry on the banner of Western civilisation which is broadly liberal, democratic and capitalistic. The society as a whole is permissive and materialistic. Thus the British education system is happy with the job of creating a rational man whose only target

is individual fulfilment. *Wahy* (revelation) does not have any place in the Western education model. Religion has been either abolished or placed as an isolated domain of knowledge which has very little to do with one's individual or collective life. Science and technology have enjoyed excessive adoration. Pride and ambition have become the prime motive for acquiring knowledge. In the recent decades 'commercialisation' has influenced the whole Western education system, including the British. The system is an effective one and also a dynamic driving force for the materialistic values, but unable to satisfy the Muslim requirement of 'the good of this world and that of the world hereafter' . . . [8]

The Islamic opposition to secular approaches to education became very evident in the response of Muslims to the concept of multiculturalism, which was popular during the 1970s and 1980s. It meant in practice that the differences between people of different religions were to be understood in terms of culture rather than religion, and that schools were seen as places where differences of culture could be recognized and celebrated. The scorn of the Muslim community for these ideas is expressed by Bari:

> The Muslim community is dismayed at the thrust of 'multiculturalism' in the state-system where 'religions are presented as a variety of customs to choose from with the effect that commitment is drowned and neutralised in plurality'. This multi-cultural or multi-faith concept 'penetrates the whole school curriculum and is often more damaging in its results than a strict Christian teaching . . .' To Muslims it is a secular concept in disguise. Their opposition to this approach is universal. [9]

Mervyn Hiskett, a writer on Islam with a particular interest in education, is equally scornful about multiculturalism:

> The fact is, multicultural education in Britain has failed because the multiculturalists have failed to understand the nature of Islam. What they offer is a gallimaufry of humanist ideas, and some highly selective comparative relativism, shorn of all 'irrational' elements, for which an unhallowed relativism, not a

passionate accession of faith and a blinding encounter with divinity, is the premise. This is defended as 'an ability to cope with the uncertainty posed by pluralism'. In fact, it is an attempt to extinguish the sacerdotal. It may seem admirable in the fashionable context of liberal doubt. But what the multiculturalists forget – or have never understood – is that the equation is altogether one-sided. For on the Islamic side there is neither doubt nor pluralism, and only very limited tolerance. If one confronts this pallid rationalist suspension of belief with the fiery afflatus of transcendental conviction, there is little doubt which will win. All that multiculturalism does is enable the Muslims to run rings round their trusting multiculturalist and inter-faith well-wishers, in the business of bending the British education system to their will.[10]

2. Muslim requests and demands

When Muslims feel that the religious and cultural needs of their children in British schools are not being adequately met, they feel obliged to make their wishes known, either in the form of 'requests' or 'demands'. A leaflet entitled *Muslim Children in British Schools: their Rights and Duties* expresses the thinking behind such requests and demands:

> This report looks at the duties Muslim children MUST observe while they are at school and the provisions that the law of this country allows them to carry out their duties. For too long Muslim parents have allowed their children to do as they please while they are at school, this always results in the children growing away from their religion and eventually rejecting their religion altogether. Until Muslims can set up their own schools they should make sure that their children are carrying out their duties as Muslims in state schools.[11]

The following are the main requests that have been made to enable Muslims to carry out these duties required by their faith:

(a) They ask for provision of *halal* food or vegetarian alternatives. Muslim children should not be asked to eat any foods that are explicitly forbidden by their religion.

(b) Permission is sought for dress that is acceptable to Muslims. Muslim girls often wish to wear the shalwar-kameez and a small headscarf. Some believe that the practice of girls wearing skirts is 'totally un-Islamic', and believe that 'parents should not under any circumstances allow their daughters to wear skirts to school'.[12] While there is no religious objection to Muslims taking part in PE or games, they often request that loose-fitting track suits should be allowed for both boys and girls. They ask that they should also be allowed to wear amulets round their necks at all times.

(c) Muslims generally demand single-sex PE and swimming for pupils above the age of 10.

(d) Washing facilities for boys and girls should always be separate. Requests are sometimes made for containers of water to be provided in each WC for the benefit of those who value 'an oriental approach to cleansing themselves'.[13] For children aged from 10 or 11, separate cubicles should be available for both boys and girls for taking showers and changing after PE and swimming, so that they are not required to shower or dress in front of each other. This is based on the Islamic belief that 'exposure of the body even to people of the same sex is unacceptable'.[14]

(e) Because certain types of music, dance and drama are regarded as offensive to some Muslim parents, children should not be asked to take part in these activities against their wishes. Mixed dancing is not encouraged at any age. Loose clothes should always be worn for dancing. Karim presents this view even more strongly: 'Dance and music are both un-Islamic activities ... All activities such as dance and music are geared to create physical attraction between boys and girls which leads to permissiveness ... Muslim parents should therefore make full use of their rights and exclude their children from activities which would affect their children adversely.'[15]

(f) Health and sex education should be taught with special sensitivity, and Muslims should exercise their right to withdraw their children from sex education if they wish. Karim explains the feelings of some Muslims: 'In Islam sex education is a field which is strictly a family affair ... Islam is totally opposed to sex education. It makes our young shameless and prevents children from developing naturally. It also removes a fundamental duty from parents. Muslims should make sure that their children are excluded from such degrading and de-humanizing lessons.'[16]

(g) A room should be available for Muslims to lay down their prayer mats and say their prayers, which would usually be during their lunch break or other breaks. There should also be appropriate facilities for the ritual ablutions before prayers. Some Muslims who believe that attendance at Friday prayers is an essential part of Islam and therefore obligatory for all Muslims encourage parents to ask for permission for children to be absent for part of Friday afternoon in order to attend mosque, or to ask for someone to come into the school to lead the prayers on Friday.

(h) The 1944 Education Act allows for children to be absent during religious festivals. Muslim pupils therefore often wish to be absent to celebrate Eid-ul-Fitr and Eid-ul-Adha. Schools are often requested to arrange holidays or teacher training days to coincide with Muslim festivals. Where this does not happen, large numbers of children tend to absent themselves from school on these days.

(i) Muslims often ask schools to provide Muslim teachers to give separate religious education to the Muslim children.

(j) Requests are sometimes made for separate collective worship for Muslims, since parents have the right to withdraw their children from collective worship if they wish. In schools where there are sizeable numbers of children of faiths other than Christianity, the 1988 Education Act allows schools to apply for a 'determination', that is, permission to hold a different form of worship either for the whole school or for a group of pupils within the school.

(k) Information should be provided by the school to answer the special questions that Muslims often ask, for example about policy on *halal* food, dress, collective worship and religious education.

(l) Books on Islam in the library and in the classroom should be authentically Islamic, or at least accurate and fair in their portrayal of Islam.

(m) Islamic studies and Arabic should be taught at GCSE and A-level standard.
(n) Methods of fund raising that are offensive to Muslims (for example lottery) should not be allowed in the school.
(o) Muslims generally press for single-sex secondary schools. This is described by M.A. Bari as 'by far the most urgent demand' of Muslim parents.[17]
(p) State-funded Muslim schools (see Section 4).
(q) Muslims would like to see a more thoroughly Islamic curriculum.

While this last point is not presented as a request to the state, it is worth recognizing the seriousness with which Muslim scholars are attempting to bring a thoroughly Islamic mind to bear on the whole subject of education and to 'think Islamically' about every area of human knowledge and science. There are interesting parallels between this attempt and the attempt of some Christians to develop a thoroughly Christian approach to education, including mathematics, history and science. The basic idea in this 'Islamization of knowledge', as explained by Syed Ali Ashraf, is

> that the Islamic concept of human nature and knowledge should form the basis of all concepts for all branches of knowledge . . . faith in and love for God and the Prophet of Islam must provide the only sustainable and permanent framework to hold unchanging values. Otherwise the evolutionary concept of values and the dependence of values on changing social scenes will destroy the basic framework and lead humanity to complete uncertainty about 'values' and the notion of the purification and improvement of the 'self'.[20]

Bari explains that most of the subjects in the normal curriculum in Britain 'are based on the secular education model of the West and are, naturally, not relevant to Islam and Muslim expectation'.[18] He gives the following as an example of an Islamic curriculum from a privately funded Muslim school, where the subjects taught are: the basic Islamic beliefs, Qur'an phonology, Islamic jurisprudence, English, Mathematics,

Science, Geography, History (general and Muslim), and languages (Arabic, Bengali and Urdu). He notes that this 'Muslim curriculum' does not include any European language, music, drama or art.[19]

3. Responses from the authorities

Head teachers and school governors have to respond to these various requests, whether they come from the parents of their pupils or from religious or community leaders. The following would seem to be some of the key factors that are likely to influence their responses.

(i)   Finance and resources

In some cases responses may be determined by financial considerations. How much would it cost, for example, to build individual cubicles and install enough showers to enable every child in a class of thirty plus to wash and change in private?

(ii)   Culture and religion

Sometimes it will be hard to work out whether one is dealing with an issue related to culture or to religion. In commenting on the desire of many Muslims to have separate cubicles for showering and changing Peter Woodward has to say, 'it may be that cultural rather than Islamic factors lie behind this'.[21] It is of course notoriously difficult to separate culture from religion when dealing with a religion that is so insistent on embracing every aspect of life. One Muslim educationist says that because Islam is 'a system that seeks to regulate all aspects of life in accordance with the values of revelation' it should be regarded, along with Judaism and Shintoism, as a *din* and not as a 'religion' like Christianity, Buddhism and Taoism.[22] Where then does one draw the line? Is everything in the lifestyle of Muslims from the Middle East or the Indian subcontinent to be regarded as 'Islamic'? If some of these requests reflect the cultural norms of a particular society rather than the religious requirements imposed on all Muslims, how far should secular authorities be obliged to go in accommodating these requests?

(iii) Prejudice

When their requests and demands are so often rejected out of hand, Muslims suspect that sometimes they are rejected out of 'apprehension, misunderstanding and . . . unfamiliarity'.[23] At other times they may feel that the reasons are more sinister, in that they arise out of racial or religious prejudice against Islam. Bari recognizes how these prejudices come into play in thinking about education:

> Islamic education is seen as theocratic, secluded and therefore irrelevant to British life-style. As such it is marred by the negative image of Islam and the Muslim people at home and abroad. To most Britons Islam itself remains a medieval Middle Eastern or Asian culture unfit to adjust to modern western life. Prejudice against Islam is a hangover from the Crusades and from the Imperial Age.[24]

(iv) Mutual respect and tolerance

Muslims are making strong pleas that school authorities show more genuine respect and tolerance for ideas and practices which may seem different and alien. These pleas need to be heard by those who are so culture-bound that they imagine that there is only one way of doing things – which must of course be the way they are familiar with in their own culture. There may be times, however, when Muslims need to be asked whether they are willing and able to practise the same kind of tolerance that they are demanding of others. If they expect others to respect deeply held Muslim convictions, are they able to show the same respect for convictions with which they profoundly disagree? If the majority community is generous and open-hearted, minorities ought to feel secure enough to show the same generosity and tolerance. A less prejudiced attitude to Islam and Muslims would mean a greater acceptance of cultural forms that appear initially to

be very foreign. Writing about the situation in Germany
Rotraud Wielandt, a professor of Islamic studies in Bavaria,
believes that the host community must be 'serious in practising the pluralism it professes in the run of everyday living in
relation to Muslims. For example, rather than a one-sided
insistence on Muslims becoming assimilated in every way to
Western norms, they should be made to feel that their own
norms are being respected.'[25]

(v)   'The thin end of the wedge'?

Those in authority may have genuine respect for the wishes of
Muslim parents and children, and genuinely want to grant
their requests as far as they can. Sometimes, however, they
may be unduly cautious about granting the request out of fear
that as soon as it has been granted, other more serious demands will follow. In some cases the caution and fear may arise
out of an awareness that behind those making the request there
are particular Muslim groups that have their own more radical
agendas that they want to press in schools. If it is felt that any
concessions are likely to be exploited, there may be a natural
reluctance to reach any accommodation.

It has to be admitted that we are dealing here with the basic
suspicion in the minds of many Europeans that alongside the
gentler and more liberal face of Islam that is so evident in
places in the West, there are other faces of Islam which are
not so tolerant and well-meaning. In the Shi'a tradition of
Islam the principle of *taqiyya*, sometimes translated 'simu-
lated submission', allows and even encourages a kind of
calculated deception, if it will enable the Muslim community
to survive in a hostile environment. What if Muslims of other
traditions sometimes work on the same principle? There is
therefore the lurking fear that while some Muslims may be
very happy to use democratic processes to gain their ends,
they may not be so committed to democracy when they are
actually in a position of power and authority.

If it seems embarrassing or disturbing to both sides to
analyse reactions to Muslim requests in this way, one can
only hope that 'naming the demons' may be the first step

towards exorcising them. The only way to work through
these fears and suspicions on both sides is to develop relationships of trust and openness in which all parties can feel
completely secure and free to speak their minds.

4. The question of state-funded Muslim schools

When requests for single-sex schools and other requests already noted meet with negative responses from local authorities, the Muslim community often feels that the only way they
can protect themselves, their religion and their culture is to
establish their own schools. In recent years the issue seems
to have become 'a political symbol . . . for Muslims, who
consider that their needs . . . have been systematically ignored
and their status undermined'.[26]

Muslims argue that the right for a religious community to
establish its own schools within the state system (known as
'voluntary-controlled schools') is enshrined in the 1944 Education Act. 'They see it as their right, not favour, enshrined in the
British law.'[27] After many unsuccessful applications, the Labour
government in January 1998 gave approval for government
funding for two Islamic schools, the Islamic School in Brent from
April 1998 and the Al-Furqan Primary School in Birmingham
from September 1998. They have found it hard to understand
why around 1,558,770 children are educated in 7,012 Anglican,
Catholic, Methodist and Jewish voluntary aided schools, but not
a single Muslim child is educated at state expense in a Muslim
school.[28] 'A fair minded person,' says M.A. Bari, 'sees no reason
why the Muslims are denied their rights when, like other
people, they pay their taxes.'[29]

While the response of many (including Christians) at the
present time is to resist such demands, a more positive approach
is to accept willingly that there is no legal reason why state
funding should not be available for Muslim schools, and then
to work through some of the implications of setting up such
schools. If the principle is accepted gladly rather than grudg-
ingly, there should be a basis for goodwill on all sides for
discussing questions like the following, which probably need to

be asked in relation to every request for a voluntary-aided Muslim school.

(a) Can this Muslim school serve the whole Muslim community? Would there be any pressure put on Muslim parents to send their children to such schools? Would there be any inclination to include only one group or sect within it? While we may have to accept the fact that denominational schools are part of our tradition in Britain, would Muslims accept the principle that we do not want any new kinds of denominationalism to be created or perpetuated within the Muslim community?

(b) What are the obligations that go with voluntary-aided status? Commitment to the National Curriculum is one of the most obvious obligations, which would generally present no problems to Muslims. The government would need to ensure that in their evaluation of Muslim schools the inspectors would not show any bias, either by unfair criticism of the schools or by applying a different set of standards to protect them from criticism.

(c) What would be the knock-on effect on other schools in the area? Would the creation of such a school take a significant number of pupils away from existing schools? It seems that in practice this is one of the hardest questions to answer, since the creation of voluntary-aided Muslim schools would in many situations have a disruptive effect on existing schools, forcing some of them to close. The question then needs to be faced whether a very considerable reorganization of schools in a wide area is a price that is worth paying to achieve the aim of Muslim schools.

(d) How would Islam and other faiths be taught? If the agreed approach to religious education in this country at present requires that children in state-funded schools should be taught about religions (including their own) in an impartial and non-confessional way, it would not be unreasonable to expect Muslim children to be introduced to other faiths in this same sympathetic but neutral way. Muslims would probably find it hard to avoid teaching Islam as if it is true. But if Christian teachers have had to wrestle for many years with the problem of how to teach Christianity in a non-confessional way – even if they are convinced of its truth – Muslim teachers would have to do the same. If it is accepted as important in a multi-faith society that people should know about the faith and practice of each other's religion, Muslim children need to be taught about Islam in the context of teaching about other faiths.

(e) Could the creation of these schools avoid 'ghetto-ization'? It is often argued that the creation of state-funded Muslim schools would have the effect of encouraging Muslim communities to become totally self-contained, with little or no desire to relate to the wider community. If in some cities Muslim communities already seem to function like ghettos in certain respects, having Muslim schools would simply perpetuate the ghetto mentality. Many believe that divisions between Protestants and Catholics in Ireland have been kept alive and hardened by separate schools, and that state-funded Muslim schools could hardly avoid perpetuating the same kind of divisions between the children of different ethnic and faith communities.

This argument is sometimes countered by pointing to the experience of Roman Catholics with their schools. The Roman Catholic bishop of Leeds, for example, has supported the Muslim demand for voluntary-aided schools in these terms: 'The experience of my own community, which had been a persecuted minority, is that having our own schools within the state system helped us to move out of our initial isolation, so as to become more confident and self-assured. The effect of separate schools for us has been integration, not divisiveness.'[30] This argument could well have considerable force if Muslims can show the whole community that they do actually want to move out of their isolation. Sadly the impression is often given by some in the Muslim community that they do *not* want to be integrated into the wider community, and are asking for state-funded Muslim schools in order to help them to be insulated from the harmful influences of secular society.

(f) Does the Muslim community have the resources and the experience to guarantee the success of the school and the quality of its work? The Muslim community would need to convince the government that they have the financial resources and the personnel required to run voluntary-aided schools. They would be required, for example, to raise 15 per cent of the capital outlay. To maintain the Muslim ethos of the school they would no doubt want to have a majority of Muslim teachers. But since there is a shortage of qualified Muslim teachers, the schools would probably be dependent on a large proportion of non-Muslim staff.

While some of these questions can easily be answered, others could raise problems that cannot easily be resolved. All of the parties involved need to be willing to make concessions. But if the principle of voluntary-aided Muslim schools is accepted, the Muslim community may perhaps be convinced of the nation's determination to be just and fair in its treatment of minorities, and we will have gone some way towards recognizing a genuine sense of grievance.

5. Collective worship in schools

The 1988 Education Reform Act requires a daily 'act of collective worship', and stipulates that it should be 'wholly or mainly of a broadly Christian character'. However easy it may be for the majority of schools to meet this requirement, it has to be acknowledged that schools where the majority of pupils are Muslims have found it to be almost totally unworkable. When so many schools are either unable or unwilling to meet the requirement for a daily act of worship, the law is quietly ignored and is thus brought into disrepute. One basic reason (which no doubt applies in schools of all kinds throughout the country) is that one cannot compel anyone to worship, and one cannot compel teachers with little or no faith of their own to lead Christian worship. Inevitably there is always going to be an element of hypocrisy in going through the motions of worship without any conviction. One further reason for unease has been that at the time when the present legislation was being proposed in the 1980s, there was a strong suspicion that government policy was motivated by a political desire to use education as a means of dealing with difficult social problems.

A further argument against the present requirement for collective worship is that it has proved in practice to be divisive. The insistence on *Christian* teaching and *Christian* worship has forced both moderates and radicals of different faiths to demand separate worship for different faith groups. If there were no such insistence on the Christian emphasis, Muslims would probably have been content to join in some kind of worship activity with the rest of the school community. Dividing pupils into different faith communities for worship sometimes has the effect of increasing tension between faith communities.

While it makes sense to allow some kind of collective worship in church schools or in independent Christian schools, it does not make sense to require it in state schools, especially where the majority of the pupils are Muslim. If the requirement for a daily act of collective worship were to be replaced by a requirement for assemblies, each school would have the freedom, through its staff, governors and parents, to work out the kind of assemblies that would be most appropriate for the school. They would need to be educational rather than confessional, with a clear understanding that there would be no attempt to commend one particular religion as 'the truth'. They could contain a certain amount of distinctively Christian content, but could also include elements from other faiths. There could be a focus on religious and moral themes acceptable to people of all faiths or none.

6. What kind of pluralism can Muslims accept?

Underlying all the individual issues already noted is the fundamental problem that Muslims find it difficult to work in a situation in which their faith is regarded as one option among many. Bari recognizes the problem when he says that 'Islamic education is seen as theocratic'.[31] This perception is entirely correct, since the secular world of the West cannot and does not accept the divine authority of the revelation on which the

Islamic approach to education is ultimately based. But if this
is the case, is there any way in which Muslims can work out
an adequate rationale for operating within the state education
system in a secular society? What kind of pluralism, if any, can
they accept?

This is the question addressed by Rotraud Wielandt in an
article on 'Islamic Religious Education in a Pluralist Society'. He
begins by acknowledging that 'Muslims share with adherents
of other world religions the conviction that their own faith is the
only one that is in the fullest sense true and universally valid.'[32]
But if Muslims recognize that they live in a very un-Islamic
situation in post-Christian Western democracies, how can they
bring themselves to accept living in a pluralist society? Speaking
about the German situation he suggests that since

> it is quite unrealistic at present to imagine that there are, or soon
> will be, mass conversions to Islam in Central and Western Europe
> . . . we should work on the assumption that for the foreseeable
> future the overwhelming majority of Turkish Muslims in Ger-
> many will be living in a climate of religious and cultural plural-
> ism. Since in the long run they will not be able to insulate
> themselves from it completely, they will therefore have to incor-
> porate it into the way they think of themselves and the world, and
> adapt to it in the way they behave.[33]

In searching for resources within the Islamic tradition that can
enable Muslims to cope with this kind of pluralism in the
context of religious education, Wielandt recognizes that some
verses in the Qur'an do seem to provide 'a basis for a positive
assessment of religious and cultural pluralism', for example:
'There is no compulsion in religion' (Q. 2:256) and 'If God had
so willed, He would have made you all one community
(*umma*)' (Q. 5:48). There are other verses, however, which
suggest a less open approach, and these are the verses that tend
to be quoted by those with less tolerant attitudes: for example,
'religion, for God, is Islam' (Q. 3:19). If we look to the practice
of the early Muslim community to provide precedents, the
tolerance extended by the first Muslims to their Jewish and
Christian subjects can hardly be used as a paradigm for today,

since 'it always presupposed a situation in which Muslims were the rulers, and Islamic law was sovereign within the state'. A more hopeful approach is to point to the diversity within Islam itself. If Muslims are prepared the live with the considerable diversity within Islam, are they not prepared to live with similar diversity among world faiths and ideologies? The problem Wielandt sees here, however, is that Muslims are often unable or unwilling to admit to this kind of 'plurality of interpretations within Islam itself'.

Wielandt concludes that the most promising starting-point for affirming pluralism within Islam lies in

> the attempt to forge links between the modern spirit of liberty, as this has achieved prominence in Europe especially since the Enlightenment, and the fundamental teachings about human nature which are to be found in the Qur'an . . . In making human beings his representative (*khalifa*) on earth (c.f. Q. 2:30), God granted them a measure of participation in the freedom involved in his own creativity, and therefore he only desires faith that has been freely chosen. Believers worldwide are faced today with the challenge of combining loyalty to their own faith community with recognition of also belonging to the larger community of all those who, like them, have reached the conclusion that they have, in the matter of faith, as the result of a conscientious struggle to discern God's will.

It will be interesting to see whether, as Wielandt hopes, Muslims themselves can go back to their sources to find ways of affirming ideas about liberty and tolerance that have been developed in the West. In view of the strong words of Nasr about the capitulation of many Muslims to the thinking of the Enlightenment (see Chapter 1), it is quite possible that the more conservative Muslims will dismiss the possibility of any such compromise with the West (see Chapter 7).

7. A new approach to religious pluralism in schools?

If secularism has not been able to provide an adequate basis for education in schools in a pluralist society, largely because it has failed to appreciate the nature of certain faiths, is it possible to work out a different kind of of consensus on which secularists, Christians and Muslims can agree? Could people of all faiths or of none accept the following propositions as a basis for working together in state schools?

(a) The task of state schools is to *educate* rather than to *convert*. Instructing children in the faith of their parents should be primarily the responsibility of parents and religious teachers in the church or the mosque. While Christianity and Islam will inevitably be taught as 'the truth' in Christian and Muslim independent schools, there is no place for this kind of catechism in state schools. Children need to know a certain amount about different faiths, especially those represented in their community and their nation. If a great deal of fear and prejudice are based on ignorance, an understanding of other faiths should help to reduce prejudice. The refusal to engage in proselytizing should apply just as much to the secularist as to the Christian or the Muslim.

(b) Children should be brought up not only to understand different faiths and ideologies, but to *respect* their beliefs and way of life, even if they disagree strongly with them. Even in the context of open discussion and critical questioning, no beliefs and ideologies should be laughed out of court and denied a fair hearing. This respect will include the recognition that a number of different faiths make very distinctive truth claims.

(c) People of all faiths and of none can come together to affirm certain basic values that they all share, like honesty, fairness, equality, unselfishness, service and so on, simply because they contribute to the well-being of society as a whole. Even when people of different faiths and ideologies differ from each other at a fairly fundamental level, there are many areas in which they can join hands and work together for the good of the community.

(d) Since Christianity is the religion that has shaped the history and culture of Britain more than any other for centuries, and since the majority of the population still expresses a preference of some kind for the Christian faith (see Chapter 7), it is not unreasonable to suggest that Christianity should continue to be recognized as the major religious tradition in Britain. If it is impossible to understand medieval Europe, the Reformation or the plays of Shakespeare without some understanding of Christianity, even history and literature need to be taught with some reference to the Christian faith. While it is conceivable that the time could come when the influence of Christian faith will be minimal in the life of the nation, there is every reason why the Christian faith should for the time being continue to maintain its somewhat privileged position in education.

If people of all faiths and of none can accept these propositions as a basis for cooperation in schools, we may have the beginnings of the kind of consensus that is proposed by Trevor Cooling, the Director of the Association of Christian Teachers. In an article entitled 'Living as a Christian in the World of Religious Education', he addresses the dilemmas faced by committed Christians in the world of religious education. The three strategies he proposes, however, could perhaps be applied not only to religious education, but to education in general. And his pleas directed to committed Christians could apply equally well to committed Muslims:

1. It must be recognized that even though we all hold our theology passionately, and this is as true of the pluralist as of the evangelical, we must accept some restraint on our desire to share our beliefs with others if we are to apply our theology in education in a way that is ethically acceptable. To ask this of someone is not to ask them to compromise, or even to change, their theology. It is rather to ask them to recognize that state funded education is a particular context, which legitimately demands restraint from believers if their theology is to be successfully contextualised within it and the diversity principle upheld ...

2. Instead of expending energy seeking to prove that any particular theology is superior as a support for education, our energies should be devoted to developing a code of conduct

which will apply to everyone teaching religious education, irrespective of their personal commitments. Then the emphasis will be on responsible behaviour in the way teachers influence their pupils, rather than on trying to decide which is the most rational theology for schools to propagate . . .

3. Finally all teachers will have to accept that religious education in state funded schools can only have limited objectives if it is not to become totalitarian. Seeking to persuade children of 'the truth', or encouraging them to hold 'beliefs more appropriate to the modern world', is the province of the voluntary faith community and not of government schools. Evangelisation by government employees in the name of education is a form of political abuse. Rather schools should concentrate on promoting the legitimate concerns of government, of which I should think one of the most important is encouraging people of different religious persuasions to cooperate with each other as fellow citizens.[34]

Conclusion

The first and most obvious conclusion we must draw is that the gap between full-blown secularism and Islam is virtually unbridgeable. Secularists rule God-talk out of any debate about education. They have no place for absolutes based on revelation, and the only basis they can accept for ethical values is personal preference, the moral consensus of any particular society or the wishes of the most powerful. When Muslims enter this secular world, they bring a world-view and a culture that, they believe, has the authority of God behind it. Is it therefore surprising that there is a fundamental clash of world-views?

Multiculturalism has failed to provide an adequate basis for education in a pluralistic society. Any philosophy of this kind that cannot allow for the possibility of a supernatural world that impinges on human beings is bound to be at a loss when confronted by the confidence and self-assurance of Muslims who believe that their religion is actually *true*, and that God makes claims on all human beings in every area of life. If Muslims and secularists are to find any common ground on which they can meet, they will have to be able to recognize and respect the nature of each other's world-view, even if they do not accept its truth.

In the encounter between Islam and Western secularism, Christians generally stand somewhat uneasily in the middle, sometimes identifying with the Muslim community, and sometimes with the secular West. At times they share the deep unease Muslims feel about a secular approach to education, and are encouraged to find fellow-believers who want to bring God into every area of public life, including the classroom. Christians may even feel shamed by the fact that Muslims are courageously saying things that they themselves should perhaps have been saying. Then again there are times when Christians feel somewhat envious, wondering why the secular world seems more prepared to respect the sensitivities of Muslims than those of the Christians. At other times, however, they feel that Muslims have only just begun to feel the cold blasts of modern scepticism that Christians have been living with in the Western world for several centuries. They also sense that in their resistance to secularization, Muslims may not always have understood it very well, and may not have learned to appreciate the positive benefits it has brought to Western society.

There is a desperate need to move from a 'culture of demand' to a 'culture of dialogue'. This can only be achieved if both sides are willing to listen to each other and enter into a relationship of real trust. Speaking about the situation in Germany, Wielandt spells out the obligations of *both* the Muslim community *and* the non-Muslim majority:

> The necessity of consciously promoting a culture of dialogue applies, in our pluralist society, not only to the religious minority in Germany, composed of Muslims from Turkey, but also to all other religious (and non-religious) groups, including those to which a large proportion of the indigenous population belongs. The Muslim minority can hardly be expected to experience pluralism as something positive, and to develop a corresponding readiness to engage in discussions with adherents of other world views, if the non-Muslim majority for its part refuses to enter into

such discussions, or is lukewarm about doing so, out of a failure to recognize (whether out of ignorance, or a sense of superiority or whatever) that the voice of Islam may have a worthwhile contribution to make to public opinion . . . members of the Islamic community have an unequivocal right, in a democracy, to inject their own particular religious beliefs and values into public debate as a contribution to the formation of a normative consensus . . . The non-Muslim majority have to face up to the question of whether, in the long term, they are capable of accepting the religion of the Muslim minority as a legitimate component of the overall political and cultural configuration of their country . . .[35]

If there is to be such a 'culture of dialogue', Christians may have a particularly important role as bridge-builders. They have had to accept, however unwillingly, the rising tides of doubt and scepticism. They know that neither parents nor clergy can tell people what to believe, or expect them to believe without asking questions. Christians have also had to accept that not everything that has come out of Western philosophy and science has been destructive of Christian faith. While resisting the atheistic and agnostic premises of the Enlightenment, they have come to welcome – sometimes rather reluctantly – many of the fruits that have come from the spirit of free inquiry and the rejection of dogmatism. In the world of education Christians have had to make significant concessions. But the accommodation reached between the churches and the secular government earlier this century enabled the churches to hold on to some kind of privileged position inherited from its earlier monopoly of education and to enter into a creative partnership with the state.

We may find in practice that while the educationists, the theologians and religious teachers sit around discussing these issues, the most significant developments within the Muslim community are being, and will continue to be, determined by young Muslims themselves. They are the ones who see all the options open to them within society and have to decide on the direction of their lives. They may be influenced more by pragmatic considerations than by religious principles, and it may be that religious teachers are followed by the young less than they think they are. Perhaps young Muslims are 'creating facts on the ground', causing a quiet revolution behind the backs of their religious leaders!

In the world of education, therefore, this is the kind of message that Christians may want to send to Muslims: 'We share your unease about the dominance of secularism in the Western world today. But we have been living with these challenges for centuries, and have constantly found ourselves walking a delicate tightrope. While we continue to challenge the secular mind at point after point, we have also learned to accept many things within the Western intellectual tradition that we believe have produced real benefits. We have tried to listen, but without losing our integrity or changing the essence of the Christian faith. So while there are areas where you still fundamentally disagree both with Christians and secularists, are there areas where you can sit down and talk, and then actually join hands and work together with us? Or do you feel that your own mission and your own agenda are so unique that you continue to see both Christianity and secularism as enemies who are stubbornly resisting your demands?'

Notes

[1] Imtiaz Karim, 'Muslim Children and British Schools: Their rights and duties', *Straight Path Monthly*, Birmingham.

[2] Mervyn Hiskett, *Some to Mecca Turn to Pray: Islamic values in the modern world*, Claridge Press, St Albans, 1993, p. 308.

[3] Rotraud Wielandt, 'Islamic Religious Education in a Pluralist Society', *British Journal of Religious Education*, vol. 15, no. 2, 1993, p. 56.

[4] Seyyed Hossein Nasr, 'Islam and the West: Yesterday and today' in *Q-News International*, no. 248–50, 27 Dec 1996–9 Jan 1997, p. 13.

[5] M.A. Bari, 'Muslim Demands for their own Denominational Schools in the United Kingdom', *Muslim Education Quarterly*, vol. 10, no. 2, 1993. p. 63.

[6] Ibid., p. 62.

[7] Ibid., p. 66.

[8] Ibid., pp. 63–4. Author's interpolation.

9   Ibid., pp. 65–6.
10 Hiskett, op. cit., pp. 308–9.
11 Karim, op. cit., p. 1.
12 Ibid., p. 3.
13 Peter Woodward, 'Muslim Pupils in British Schools: Our questions, their answers', *Muslim Education Quarterly*, vol. 10, no. 2, 1993, p. 43.
14 Ibid.
15 Karim, op. cit., p. 4.
16 Ibid.
17 Bari, op. cit., p. 67.
18 Ibid., p. 64.
19 Ibid., p. 68.
20 Syed Ali Ashraf, John Shortt and Trevor Cooling (eds.), *Agenda for Educational Change*, Apollos, 1997, p. 272.
21 Woodward, op. cit., p. 44.
22 Yaqub Zaki, 'The Teaching of Islam in Schools: A Muslim viewpoint', *British Journal of Religious Education*, vol. 5, no. 1, 1982, p. 36.
23 Bari, op. cit., p. 70.
24 Ibid., p. 69.
25 Wielandt, op. cit., p. 55.
26 *Schools of Faith: Religious schools in a multicultural society*, Commission for Racial Equality, 1990, quoted in an unpublished paper by Philip Lewis on 'The Establishment of Muslim Voluntary-Aided Schools'.
27 Bari, op. cit., p. 70.
28 Times Educational Supplement.
29 Bari, op. cit., p. 67.
30 *Bradford Telegraph and Argus*, 3 January 1991, quoted in Philip Lewis, op. cit.
31 Bari, op. cit., p. 69.
32 Wielandt, op. cit., p. 50.
33 Ibid., p. 51.
34 Trevor Cooling, 'Living as a Christian in the World of Religious Education', *Religious Education*, vol. 12, no. 2, 1990, pp. 29–35.
35 Wielandt, op. cit., pp. 56–7.

Seven

Establishment: Does the Islamic Presence Alter the Equation?

Introduction

Serious religion . . . is tolerated only if completely divorced from public life . . . (Seyyed Hossein Nasr).[1]

The logic of privatising Christianity, of taking religion out of the public arena, disqualifies Westerners from dealing in any effective sense with Muslim theocratic demands (Lamin Sanneh).[2]

Faced with Britain's new ethno-religious pluralism, the question should not be 'what do we need to get rid of in order to give expression to this pluralism?', but rather, 'what do we need to create or preserve in order to have a healthy pluralism and to give institutional recognition to it?' (Tariq Modood).[3]

If Britain is now a multi-faith society, what kind of relationship should there be (if any) between all the different faith communities and the state? And in particular is it appropriate for one particular denomination, the Church of England, to hold on to its position as the established church? After outlining what is involved in the special relationship between church and state in Britain, we rehearse briefly some of the arguments that have been used for and against establishment. We then ask whether the presence in Britain of a considerable number of Muslims and people of other faiths should change the nature of the debate.

1. What is 'establishment'?

Writing in 1984 in an introduction to Max Warren's lectures on *The Functions of a National Church*, Raymond Johnston outlined what establishment involves in practice:

(a) the monarch is the 'Supreme Governor of Church and State' who appoints bishops and archdeacons;
(b) the parish system gives parishioners 'certain rights to the church's ministrations';
(c) there is an 'interlocking of Parliament and the General Synod in ecclesiastical legislation';
(d) certain bishops have the right to sit in the House of Lords;
(e) chaplains are provided for the armed services, hospitals, prisons and borstals;
(f) there is 'the national commitment to the Christian religion' expressed in various Education Acts.

Johnston went on to explain:

> These are the visible signs of the 'establishment'. They are a whole series of legal and social arrangements, at first sight unconnected. But all are rooted in historical events and institutions which have shaped the British people. They are far from being co-ordinated. They have been subject to erosion and adjustment in detail. They will go on changing. But they continue to mark out the nation's life as Christian in some sense doubtless a weaker sense than we often attach to that adjective.[4]

This relationship between church and state in Britain is unique, although there are some parallels to certain aspects of the relationship in Germany and Scandinavia. While it has developed and been modified over centuries, it has for some years been challenged by people of very different political and religious persuasions.

2. The question of statistics

If both of the main sides of the argument appeal to statistics to support their case, how in practice are we to use the statistics concerning the different faith communities?

(i) Christian churches

The question that needs to be asked here is what criteria should we use to determine adherence to the Christian faith? What proportion of the population consider themselves to be 'Christian' in any sense, or would consider themselves to be related to the Church of England?

(a) If we settle for some kind of belief in God, the European Values Systems Study concludes that in 1990 71 per cent of the population of Britain acknowledged belief in God and 76 per cent in Europe as a whole.[5]

(b) If we use occasional church attendance, the European Study suggests that 13 per cent of the population in Britain attend church weekly and 10 per cent monthly, with 13 per cent attending at Christmas and Easter and 8 per cent once a year.

(c) If we take into account the number of baptized people, it is estimated that in 1994 25,419,000 out of a total population in England of around 48,600,000 had been baptized in the Church of England.[6] Fifty-four per cent of all children born in the UK in 1995 were baptized in a Christian church.[7]

(d) If we include statistics for weddings and funerals, we find that in 1995, 47 per cent of all weddings took place in a church or some kind of religious building, and over two-thirds of all deaths are cremated. Peter Brierley points out that 'virtually all of these will have a religious ceremony, based on Christian prayers' and concludes that 'in the major passages of life, birth, marrige and death, Christianity plays a significant role for at least half of the population'.[8]

(e) If we look for evidence of greater commitment and ask for the numbers of *active church members*, 13.9 per cent of adults in the UK in 1994 were active church members of a variety of different churches.[9] The average Sunday attendance at Anglican churches is 2.4 per cent of the population of England. The attendance at Christmas Communion services is 4 per cent of the population aged 15 and over.[10]

Perhaps the most significant statistic of all, however, in this debate is the figure of 65 per cent, which is given in the new edition of the UK Christian Handbook as the percentage of the

Religious Community

Table 1 — Total Religious Community in millions

	1975	1980	1985	1990	1992	1994	1995[1]	2000[1]	2005[1]	2010[1]
Anglican[2]	28.2[3]	27.7[3]	27.1	26.6	26.4	26.2	26.1	25.6	25.1	24.6
Baptist[5]	0.6	0.6	0.6	0.6	0.6	0.6	0.6	0.6	0.6	0.6
Roman Catholic[2]	5.6[3]	5.7[3]	5.6	5.6	5.6	5.7	5.7	5.8	5.8	5.8
Independent[5]	0.5	0.5	0.5	0.4	0.4	0.4	0.4	0.4	0.4	0.4
Methodist	1.5	1.4	1.4	1.4	1.4	1.3	1.3	1.3	1.3	1.2
New Churches[5]	0.0	0.1	0.2	0.3	0.3	0.3	0.3	0.4	0.5	0.5
Orthodox	0.4	0.4	0.4	0.5	0.5	0.5	0.5	0.5	0.5	0.6
Other Churches[5]	0.3	0.3	0.3	0.2	0.2	0.2	0.2	0.2	0.2	0.2
Pentecostal[5]	0.2	0.3	0.3	0.3	0.3	0.4	0.4	0.4	0.5	0.5
Presbyterian[5]	2.9[3]	2.8[3]	2.7[3]	2.7[3]	2.7[3]	2.6	2.6	2.6	2.5	2.5
TOTAL Trinitarian Churches	40.2	39.8	39.1	38.6	38.4	38.2	38.1	37.8	37.4	36.9
Church of Scientology	0.1[3]	0.2[3]	0.3[3]	0.3[3]	0.3	0.4	0.5	0.6	0.8	1.0
Other non-Trinitarian Churches[5]	0.6[3]	0.6[3]	0.7[3]	0.8[3]	0.8[3]	0.8	0.8	0.8	0.9	1.0
Hindus	0.3[3]	0.4[3]	0.4[3]	0.4	0.4	0.4	0.4	0.5	0.5	0.6
Jews[5]	0.4	0.3[3]	0.3	0.3	0.3	0.3	0.3	0.3	0.3	0.3
Muslims	0.4[3]	0.6[3]	0.9[4]	1.0[3]	1.1	1.2	1.2	1.4	1.6	1.7
Sikhs[5]	0.2	0.3[3]	0.3[3]	0.5	0.5	0.5	0.6	0.6	0.7	0.8
Other religions	0.1	0.2	0.3	0.3	0.3	0.3	0.3	0.3	0.4	0.4
TOTAL non-Trinitarian and other religions	2.1	2.6	3.2	3.6	3.7	3.9	4.1	4.5	5.2	5.8
TOTAL all religions	42.3	42.4	42.3	42.2	42.1	42.1	42.2	42.3	42.6	42.7
Percentage of population:										
Trinitarian Churches	72%[3]	71%[3]	69%[3]	67%[3]	66%	65%	65%	63%	62%	60%
Non-Trinitarian churches and other religions	4%	5%	6%[3]	6%	6%	7%	7%	8%	9%	10%
Total all religions	76%[3]	76%[3]	75%[3]	73%[3]	72%	72%	72%	71%	71%	70%

[1] Estimate [2] Baptized membership [3] Revised figure [4] 852,900 more exactly [5] Taken as approximately double membership [6] Based on the estimated baptized population in 1991 of 1.9 million for the Church of Scotland, the Northern Ireland 1991 Population Census, and twice the membership of all other Presbyterian Churches, giving a Community figure of 2.7 million in 1991

Used with the permission of Peter Brierley, Christian Research, London and the Publisher, Paternoster Publishing, Carlisle. Table taken from *UK Christian Handbook 1996–7*, p. 283.

population with some kind of Christian association. In a table with the heading *Composition of religious disposition of the UK population 1995*, the percentage for 'Christians' is given as 65 per cent, for 'non-religious' as 28 per cent, and 7 per cent for 'other religions' (of which 4.88 per cent are other faiths and 2.2 per cent are non-trinitarian churches).[11] This suggests that almost two-thirds of the population have some kind of connection with the Christian church. Even if this number includes many who might be described as 'nominal' or 'notional' Christians, the number is still significant in this debate, since this is how people of all faith communities, including Muslims, count their adherents.

(ii) Other faith communities

The most reliable estimate of the number of Muslims in the UK in 1997 was between 1.2 and 1.4 million.[12] It is estimated that of the 1.2 million Muslims, 575,000 were considered 'active members'.[13]

3. General arguments for and against establishment

There are four main arguments that have been used in support of establishment:

(a) Christianity is still numerically the largest religion in the country.
(b) For around fourteen hundred years Christianity has been the dominant religious tradition in this country.
(c) Establishment recognizes that the church does not exist for itself, but to serve the nation.
(d) Establishment gives the churches opportunities to minister to people and to commend the Christian faith in ways that would not otherwise be possible.

These arguments are summed up by Johnston as follows:

> If we are willing to concede that the ethos of the nation is in any sense Christian, and that there is a real usefulness in the state's

recognition of a particular form of expression of the Christian religion, then we have identified the basic justification for the position of the Church of England as 'established' ... It is entirely appropriate that a nation whose life has been shaped by the spiritual and moral priorities of the Gospel should find that the historic church in its midst leads a life which is institutionally intertwined with that of the whole community.[14]

This is how Adrian Hastings, a Roman Catholic lay theologian, sums up the argument:

The point is that while the survival of the formality of establishment has ceased seriously to threaten the freedom of the Church or its ability to call the tune in its relationship with the state, establishment is still there to assert constitutionally, publicly and symbolically the Church's relevance both to public policy and to the care of the most needy, in prison, mental hospitals, or wherever ... What matters most in all this is that the idea that religion is a mere private matter for modern society (easily implied in formal disestablishment) has been avoided and the tradition of the Church's public responsibility maintained ...[15]

The commonest arguments against establishment are these:

(a) Christianity is now very much a minority religion. While there are many who profess some kind of nominal attachment to Christianity, the number of practising Christians is quite small. Christianity is only one of a number of faiths. There are probably as many Muslims as there are Methodists.

(b) The Christian faith has been decisively rejected in the intellectual life of the nation.

(c) Identification with the state presents Christians with impossible moral dilemmas and inevitably involves compromises. What kind of message is communicated, for example, when bishops are required to bless battleships or nuclear weapons?

(d) Separation of church and state would remove the element of hypocrisy and pretence and enable the Christian church to take more seriously its task of evangelizing the nation.

Bishop Colin Buchanan concludes that for reasons of this kind establishment represents 'a privilege we no longer deserve and a burden we don't want to bear'.[16]

4. What difference does the presence of other faith communities make?

The arguments outlined above do not take into consideration the fact that in 1994, 7 per cent of the population of England belonged to faith communities other than Christianity. When their presence is taken into the equation, it is often argued that because of establishment Christianity and the Anglican Church in particular enjoy a privileged status that is a legacy of British history, but that can no longer be justified on the basis of numbers. Ninian Smart, for example, believes that establishment makes non-Anglicans and people of other faiths into second-class citizens:

> The symbolism of the Queen as Head of the Church means that other religions, even if more vigorous, have the appearance of being second class – Catholicism, Judaism, Methodism, Nonconformist varieties, Sikhism, Islam, Hinduism and so forth . . . What the situation presents, albeit in a rather muddled way, is the identification of official religion with the supreme symbol of national identity and loyalty. In events such as Coronations, Royal Weddings, we see celebrated traditional English or British nationalism, which has no explicit place for the 'new British', that is for people who are citizens but historically have connections to religious and cultural traditions outside of the British Isles.[17]

Further examples of this argument are quoted by Tariq Modood, formerly of the Policy Studies Institute in London, and now a Professor in the Department of Sociology in the University of Bristol, in a paper entitled 'Ethno-Religious Minorities, Secularism and the British State':

> The argument is that the institutional privileging of one group is ipso facto a degrading of all others. Thus, Professor Bhikhu, a

distinguished Deputy Chairman of the Commission for Racial Equality in the 1980s, has argued that 'full citizenship [includes] the right to share the public culture' and, therefore, to ground the public culture in Christianity is to treat non-Christians as second-class citizens. Similarly, Gita Saghal and Nira Yuval-Davis argue that establishment 'assumes a correspondence between national and religious identity which marginalises non-established churches, and especially non-Christians as only partial members of the British national collectivity. They are defined to a lesser or greater extent as outsiders'.[18]

It must surely be significant, however that many voices from within other faith communities are still strongly in favour of establishment. There seem to be at least three arguments put forward to support this view.

Firstly, it is argued that establishment somehow enables people of *all* faith communities to stand together in their opposition to a somewhat arrogant and assertive secularism that dismisses all religion as irrelevant. Both the present and former chief rabbis, for example, have supported establishment. Thus Jonathan Sacks in his 1990 Reith Lectures argued strongly against disestablishment, suggesting that it would mean 'a significant retreat from the notion that we share any values and beliefs at all'.[19] For reasons of this kind Modood concludes:

> It may well be the case that an Anglican centre looks far less intimidating to the new faiths than a triumphal secularism; indeed, that the continuing establishment may even be seen as some slight counterweight to the secular hegemony and that proposals to dismantle establishment in the name of multi-faithism must be viewed as disingenuous.[20]

Secondly, establishment is said to make it considerably easier for dialogue to be maintained between secularists and people of different faiths. It could be argued that there are certain parallels between disestablishment and multiculturalism. If multiculturalism created a situation in education in which Muslims felt they could not be heard or understood, disestablishment similarly would create a situation in which Muslims and people of other faiths would have to argue their case with secular authorities who have little or no sympathy with their religious beliefs. Establishment, however, expresses the conviction that religious convictions are not ruled out of court in issues of public life, but are to be respected and taken seriously. People of all faiths and ideologies have the right to argue their case in the public arena.

Thirdly, it is claimed that establishment makes it easier for us as a nation to appreciate the nature of Islam and to negotiate with Muslims. Lamin Sanneh has pointed out that the secular West finds it almost impossible to come to terms with 'Muslim theocratic demands'.[21] Any kind of secularism that is based on agnosticism and individualism is at a loss when confronted by the demands of a whole religious community that believes itself to be based on divine revelation. Establishment, however, ensures that agnosticism and individualism are not taken to their logical conclusion, and recognizes that the majority still express a preference, however vague and inarticulate, for the Christian faith. The fact that the Christian religion is recognized as the dominant religion in the country makes it easier for an open and honest debate with the Muslim community to take place, which by its very nature seeks to function as a community of faith and not as a collection of individuals.

Conclusion

No one is likely to defend every single aspect of this 'whole series of legal and social arrangements' that together make up establishment. There are strong arguments for removing anomalies and allowing it to develop in different ways. Many, for example, would argue that representatives of other major Christian denominations and of all the major faith communities should be able to sit alongside bishops in the House of Lords. But it is hard to improve on the middle course commended by Tariq Modood, the Muslim writer already quoted:

With most constitutional reform issues . . . serious thought consists in charting a middle course between an unacceptable status

quo and an unacceptable radicalism . . . If . . . political options
were to be opened out, in addition to an exclusive 'establishment'
and disestablishment one would also have to consider the possibility of an organic evolutionary development (of the type that
the English constitution is supposed to be famous for) out of
current trends where the Church of England comes to share the
privileges of establishment but retains at least for the time being
a 'mother hen' primacy . . .[22]

Notes

[1] Seyyed Hossein Nasr, 'Islam and the West: Yesterday and today',
    Q-News International, no. 248–50, 27 Dec 1996–9 Jan 1997, p. 13.

[2] Lamin Sanneh, 'Can a House Divided Stand? Reflections on
    Christian-Muslim encounter in the West', *International Bulletin of
    Missionary Research*, Oct 1993, p. 164.

[3] Tariq Modood, 'Ethno-Religious Minorities, Secularism and
    the British State', paper presented to the Conference *Religion
    in the Common European Home*, April 1992, St Mary's College,
    London.

[4] Raymond Johnston in Max Warren and Raymond Johnston, *The
    Functions of a National Church*, Latimer House, Oxford, 1984,
    pp. 8ff.

[5] Sheila Ashford and Noel Timms, *What Europe Thinks: a study of
    Western European values*, Dartmouth, 1992, quoted in 'Belief and
    Church Attendance', *Quadrant*, Christian Research Association,
    July 1997, p. 1.

[6] Peter Brierley (ed.), *UK Christian Handbook 1996/1997*, p. 280.

[7] Brierley, *UK Christian Handbook: Religious trends 1997–98*

[8] Ibid.

[9] Brierley, *UK Christian Handbook*, op. cit., p. 240.

[10] *Church Statistics (1991)*, Central Board of Finance of the Church of
    England.

[11] Peter Brierley, *UK Christian Handbook 1997/1998*.

[12] *Islamophobia: A challenge for us all*, The Runnymede Trust, 1997,
    p. 65.

[13] The footnote in the 1996/1997 *UK Christian Handbook* p. 283
    outlines the problem surrounding these statistics: 'Community

taken as 1.15 million. This figure is disputed and estimates range from 1,070,000 (Prof Ceri Peach, 1995), and 1.5 million (Mohamed Anwar, *Muslims in Britain: 1991 census and other statistical sources*, OSIC Papers no. 9, Sept 1993) to 2.5 million to 3 million (The Muslim Parliament, 1994).'

[14] Johnston, op. cit., p. 14.
[15] Adrian Hastings, 'Church and State', the Gore Lecture given at Westminster Abbey, 13 Nov 1991, *Theology*, May/June 1992, pp. 170–1.
[16] Colin Buchanan in a presentation at the Evangelical Anglican Assembly, May 1992.
[17] Ninian Smart, 'Church, Party and State' in *Religion, State and Society in Modern Britain*, Paul Badham (ed.), Macmillan, 1987, pp. 385 and 390.
[18] Tariq Modood, op. cit.
[19] Lamin Sanneh, 'Can a House Divided Stand? Reflections on Christian-Muslim Encounter in the West, *International Bulletin of Missionary Research*, October 1993, p. 164.
[20] Modood, op. cit., p. 11.
[21] Lamin Sannah, op. cit.
[22] Ibid., p. 23.

Eight

Hopes for the Future: Dialogue on a More Level Playing Field?

> The only alternative available to mankind is dialogue in a framework of contact, communication and the free exchange of ideas. It is only through search, debate and dialogue that different moral, social and cultural alternatives can be presented in the world of today and appropriate choices made . . . Today dialogue is taking place not only in particular parts of the world, but almost everywhere. All over the world people are free to search and choose (Khurshid Ahmad).[1]

If dialogue is a conversation between two people, it clearly works best when there is some kind of equality between them and they are on roughly the same level. If one party is significantly more powerful than the other, the element of freedom and spontaneity is greatly reduced and the dialogue becomes much more difficult. Sadly this is exactly what has happened so often in the history of relationships between Islam and the West. Dialogue seldom takes place on a level playing field.

Seyyed Hossein Nasr's article, 'Islam and the West: Yesterday and today', in *Q News International* in December 1996 (quoted in Chapter 1) was illustrated by an eleventh-century painting of a Christian and a Muslim sitting in a tent, facing each other across a table and playing chess. Underneath is the caption: 'This picture of a Christian and a Muslim playing chess beautifully illustrated the kind of integration which appalled newly-arrived Crusaders.'[2] The picture clearly reflected a feeling at the time it was painted that Christians and

Muslims could face each other as equals, and the editor of the article no doubt used it as an expression of Nasr's hope that this kind of equality and integration might be recovered today.

We saw in Chapter 1 that there *have* been times in Europe and the middle East when Christendom and the House of Islam felt that they were reasonably equally matched, at least on the military level. There are some examples of other situations in the past and present where there has been a similar kind of balance. In parts of west and east Africa, for example, Christians and Muslims have often been able to live peacefully with each other and have even intermarried. When Lebanon was established as an independent country in 1942, the unwritten constitution attempted to maintain a kind of balance between the Christian and Muslim communities by having 99 deputies in the parliament divided on the ratio of five Christians to four Muslims to reflect the proportions of the two communities, established through an earlier census. This uneasy balance was maintained until it was upset by the years of civil war which began in 1975.

In most situations, however, in which Muslims and Christians have lived side by side over the centuries, there hasn't been anything like the same kind of balance between the two communities. One community, either the Christians or the Muslims, has generally been in a position of power over the other. The Christian subjects in the early Islamic Empire, for example, formed a huge majority, living under Muslim rule; but within a period of 300 years they were reduced to the position of a minority. Fifteen million Christians in the Arab world today are very conscious of their minority status, and Christians in the Sudan have suffered from the Islamic government seeking to impose a policy of Islamization. In Malaysia, while the Christian minority are free to practise their religion, opportunities for dialogue with the Muslim majority are limited.

On the other hand, the Muslims of India, after enjoying centuries of supremacy under Mughal Emperors, found themselves under the power of the British for 150 years. The Muslims of Mindanao in the south of the Philippines are a minority community who have been exploited for many years by the Roman Catholic Christian majority. In Bosnia the

Muslims feel they have been betrayed by Western powers who have given in too easily to the Orthodox Serbs. And Muslim minorities in Europe from many different ethnic backgrounds – north African, Turkish, Arab, Pakistani, Bangladeshi, and so on – generally feel relatively secure, but are very conscious of their lack of political power.

The earlier engagement between Islam and the Christian West has turned into a meeting between an Islam that has many different faces and a West with many different faces – some still Christian and some decidedly secular. And it has to be acknowledged that this meeting does not seem to be taking place on a level playing field. In spite of the fact that around fifty Muslim countries have gained independence since the Second World War, and in spite of perceptions in the West about the power of the Muslim world, Muslims themselves do not feel they are in a position of strength. They feel on the contrary that they are weak, politically, economically and culturally (see Chapter 1).

If this is the context in which Islam and the West face each other today, is there any reason for hoping that an intensified dialogue in the coming years could be more fruitful? Are there reasons for believing that in spite of all the inequalities that affect relations between Muslims and non-Muslims in different parts of the world, the meeting between Islam and the West at the present time creates unique opportunities for engagement which may never have existed before in quite the same form? Our survey of a wide range of subjects – the history of Muslim–Christian relations, the spread of Islam, conversion to Islam in Europe today, theological discussion between Muslims and Christians, Islamic responses to human rights, Muslim responses to the education system and church–state relations in Britain – suggests seven reasons for believing that there *is* something special about the possibilities for relations between Muslims and the West at the present time.

(i) We are not dealing with a straightforward dialogue between two parties, but between three or more

If in the past the major parties confronting each other were Christendom and Islam, we now have three major parties –

Christianity, Islam and (if we can continue to use the word as a kind of shorthand) secularism. But even this is a gross over-simplification, since 'Islam' is no more monolithic than 'Christianity' or 'the West'. It presents such a variety of different faces that no individual or group can claim to be speaking for 'Islam', just as no individual person or institution can claim to be speaking for 'Christianity'. The Western world appears to Muslims to be a strange amalgam of the Christian and the secular, and as Nasr recognizes, 'much of the dialogue carried out between Christians and Muslims today is coloured by the presence of that silent third partner: anti-religious secularism'.[3] The complexity of the situation certainly acts as a great leveller, and thoughtful Muslims will find it difficult to evade a closer encounter with the Christian mind, the secular mind and with everything that makes up life in the West today.

(ii) The most important and productive dialogue that is taking place is not determined by a theological agenda, but by human issues that arise out of the social contexts in which we live

Are Muslim governments, for example, willing to accept what are increasingly being seen as international norms of human rights, and are Western governments as good at respecting human rights as they claim to be? How are believers, Christian and Muslim, to educate their children in a secular society? Parents meeting each other at the school gates, teachers and school governors working in mixed schools, and social workers and community leaders involved in regeneration projects in the inner cities – all of these may be engaging in more effective and significant dialogue than theologians and apologists who can only debate about the trinity or the 'corruption' of the Bible. And in many of these situations women are much better at dialogue than men, because their dialogue usually involves the whole person and not just the intellect.

(iii)   Because of the power of the media, events in one part
of the world can have an immediate impact on relations
between Muslims and non-Muslims in other parts of the
world

The publication of Salman Rushdie's *Satanic Verses* led to a
public burning of the book in Bradford and the murder of people
associated with its publication in other parts of the world. The
Ayatollah's *fatwa* continues to sour relations between Britain
and Iran. The Gulf War was perceived by Muslims all over the
world as a war between the Christian West and the Muslim East
which revived the spirit of the Crusades. The Muslims of Birmingham are very aware of what has happened to the Muslims
of Bosnia, and fear that it may be their own turn before long to
suffer from what they see as the indifference and bias of European governments. And when all the inhabitants of Shanti
Nagar, a Christian village in Pakistan, had their homes set on
fire and their churches destroyed in February 1997, Muslim and
Christian leaders in Bradford wrote to the Pakistani High Com-
missioner in London condemning the attack and requesting
compensation for the Christian community. They understood
only too well the harmful effects that such incidents could have
on the mutual understanding and trust which have been built
up over recent years. However much they may be guilty of bias
and the perpetuation of stereotypes, the media continue to play
an important role in turning the spotlight on areas of tension
and conflict in our global village, and also on areas of common
concern.

(iv)   There is a greater willingness in the host communities
in Europe to engage in dialogue

The people of the West have tended to see Islam as a foreign
culture and an alien religion, and to think (at least privately)
'What right do they have to be here? They're coming to take
over!' Westerners often react with defensiveness and compla-
cency when these 'intruders' refuse to adapt to the ways of the
West and seem to be making more and more demands. It does
seem, though, that the host communities are gradually being

drawn – however reluctantly – into some kind of dialogue with Muslims. As they do so, the challenge they face all over Europe and the USA is well summed up in Wielandt's call for 'a culture of dialogue' which is based on his analysis of the situation in Germany:

> The Muslim minority can hardly be expected to experience pluralism as something positive, and to develop a corresponding readiness to engage in discussions with adherents of other world views, if the non-Muslim majority for its part refuses to enter into such discussions, or is lukewarm about doing so, out of a failure to recognise (whether out of ignorance, or a sense of superiority or whatever) that the voice of Islam may have a worthwhile contribution to make to public opinion . . . members of the Islamic community have an unequivocal right, in a democracy, to inject their own particular religious beliefs and values into public debate as a contribution to the formation of a normative consensus . . . The non-Muslim majority have to face up to the question of whether, in the long term, they are capable of accepting the religion of the Muslim minority as a legitimate component of the overall political and cultural configuration of their country . . .[4]

The response of the authorities to issues raised by Muslims both in education and in government suggests that there is *some* willingness to engage in this kind of dialogue (see Chapters 6 and 7). Admittedly there is still a long way to go, since prejudices based on ignorance and fear do not vanish overnight. But there does seem to be a greater willingness among people throughout the West to accept Muslims, in Wielandt's words, as 'a legitimate component of the overall political and cultural configuration of their country'.

(v)   Some Muslims seem more open to dialogue and are themselves calling for more dialogue

Both the articles quoted in Chapter 1, 'Islam and the West: Yesterday and today' by Seyyed Hossein Nasr, and 'Islam and the West: Confrontation or co-operation?' by Khurshid Ahmad, are strong pleas for more dialogue between Islam and the West. They challenge many of the typical assumptions of the West about Islam, and set out clearly the frame of mind in which they believe Muslims should be approaching the dialogue. There are of course other Muslim voices from more conservative and traditional theologians and from groups like the Muslim Brotherhood and Hizb-ut-Tahrir which are much more strident and aggressive, and have no time for dialogue. Perhaps only time will tell how the struggle between the conservatives, the moderates and the radicals within Islam will develop. Cynics might say that 'dialogue' tends to be a pastime for Western liberals (especially Christians), and that Muslims generally are very cool in their response to initiatives which always tend to come from outside. But the willingness of a growing number of Muslims to engage in dialogue rather than simply to proclaim Islam must surely be seen as a significant development in recent years.[5]

(vi) The freedom of Western society encourages greater openness in debate

If dissidents from Islamic countries exploit the lack of government censorship in the West, this freedom also makes it easier for the moderates on all sides to engage in dialogue in a way that is not often possible in Muslim countries. It is hardly an accident that people can often have much more open and frank dialogue with Arab Muslims visiting or living in the West than they ever can in the middle East. The traditions of academic scholarship also encourage a rigorous critique of *all* traditions, whether religious or secular, and make it possible to say things, both in private and in public, which cannot often be said in countries where there isn't the same kind of freedom.

(vii) There is a growing awareness that the alternatives to dialogue are too frightening to contemplate

Mere 'proclamation' (by Muslims or Christians) which is nothing more than monologue without any desire to listen or to understand will take us back to the spirit of conflict and competition which has often existed in the past. Dreams of world domination will lead to a continuation of the old struggles for political power in which the search for truth was inevitably a casualty. Wherever any of the different varieties of fundamentalism gain power (whether Christian, Muslim or secular), they can only stifle freedom and lead to new forms of repression. Khurshid Ahmad is very aware that we are standing at a crossroads, with only two possibilities open to us for the future:

> Islam and the Western world today once again seem to be in a position to approach each other on a moral and ideological plane and, as such, be a source of strength to each other in a common struggle against those forces destined to destroy human civilization. This is not the only choice. The other path of confrontation and clash is also very much available.[6]

What then are we to conclude about the three possible options included in our title – 'conflict', 'coexistence' or 'conversion'? If writers like Nasr and Ahmad represent a consensus among moderate Muslims, we can all be assured that there is no need for conflict, and no reason why there cannot be peaceful coexistence between Islam and the West. What could be clearer than Nasr's statement, 'The Islamic world cannot and does not threaten the West militarily, politically, or even economically in any conceivable way'? If we recognize the enormous differences between individual Muslims and between Muslim countries all over the world, we must cease thinking in terms of a united, monolithic religion which has a carefully worked out strategy for world domination.[7] And if we give up talking about 'Islam' and talk instead about 'Muslims', we will soon realize that 'Islam' can all too easily become an abstraction which bears little or no relationship to what is actually there on the ground in front of us.[8]

The problem for many in the West, however, is that they hear so many Muslims expressing strong hostility towards the West and everything that it stands for. Moderate Muslims distance themselves from these voices by saying, 'This is not true Islam', and point out that the hostility has more to do with politics and history than with religion. Non-Muslims,

194   *Islam and the West*

however, are left confused, wondering whether it is the radicals or the moderates who represent more faithfully the true spirit of Islam.

And what are we to think about the possibilities of 'conversion' – or at least of significant changes in attitude? Although the majority in the secular West will continue to find it difficult to appreciate a religion based on a divinely revealed law, some may at least develop a greater respect for certain aspects of Islamic belief and culture, especially if the foundations of Western culture are further eroded. Individuals will no doubt continue to accept Islam for a variety of reasons, though probably not in large numbers (see Chapter 3), and some Muslims will continue to justify their presence in Europe and the USA in terms of mission, seeking, in Isma'il al-Faruqi's words, to 'save the West'. Other Muslims, however, will be more concerned to keep their communities together and to keep their faith intact, relying on the silent witness of their lifestyle to commend their faith to others, but not entertaining great hopes for conversion to Islam. It will be interesting to see whether Muslims are able to distinguish more carefully between secularism (the philosophy that is based on a denial of the existence of God) and secularization (the social and political process), and whether they can recognize some of the good things that have come out of the latter.

Christians for their part cannot fail to be constantly challenged by Muslims, not least by their disciplined devotion, their sense of the unity of everything in life, their commitment to the family and the community, and their desire to see the authority of God recognized in the public sphere. They will also need to address more carefully the social and political issues in the West where Muslims feel there are questions of justice and equality at stake. In doing so they may be surprised to find areas in public life where they have a great deal in common with Muslims and can join hands to work together – even if this leads at times to strange alliances.[9]

Christians who have a sympathetic but critical understanding of Islam may also continue to hope that living and working with Muslims may remove some of the common misunderstandings about the Christian faith, and that individuals may perhaps come to see Jesus, son of Mary, as 'more than a prophet'. They may even dare to hope that the faith of Islam may somehow develop and change and become more gentle and open.

Any book about Islam cannot simply be about history, politics and society, and must inevitably bring God into the equation. If, of course, there is no God, then Christians and Muslims are misguided, and atheists are right in believing that there is nothing to dread or to look forward to beyond the grave. But if, as the Qur'an proclaims, our 'final return' is to God, then all of us from East and West, of every faith and of none, will one day find ourselves confronted by him. All will then be revealed about how we have responded to the truth that God has revealed, and how we have treated our neighbours in a world of suffering and injustice. We will also know which of the two faiths has grasped more clearly the way that God has chosen to reveal his will and to respond to human wrongdoing and evil.

In the meantime all of us who believe in God – both Christians and Muslims – have a huge agenda in trying to understand one another and live together in the variety of political and social contexts in which we find ourselves.

Notes

[1] Khurshid Ahmad, 'Islam and the West: Confrontation or co-operation?', *Muslim World*, vol. LXXXV, no. 1–2, Jan–April 1995, p. 71.
[2] Seyyed Hossein Nasr, 'Islam and the West: Yesterday and today', *Q News International*, no. 248–50, 27 Dec 1996–9 Jan 1997, p. 13.
[3] Ibid., p. 13.
[4] Rotraud Wielandt, 'Islamic Religious Education in a Pluralist Society', *British Journal of Religious Education*, vol. 15, no. 2, Spring 1993, p. 57.
[5] See for example Ata'ullah Siddiqui, *Christian-Muslim Dialogue in the Twentieth Century*, Macmillan, Basingstoke, 1997.
[6] Ahmad, op. cit., p. 63.
[7] See Fred Halliday, *Islam and the Myth of Confrontation: Religion and politics in the middle East*, I.B. Travis, London & New York, 1995

and John L. Esposito, *The Islamic Threat: Myth or reality?*, Oxford University Press, 1995 for helpful attempts to challenge the language of 'confrontation'.

8 It is noteworthy that two recent books make this shift in their titles: Kate Zebiri, *Muslims and Christians Face to Face*, One World, Oxford, 1997, and Hugh Goddard, *Christians and Muslims: From double standards to mutual understanding*, Curzon Press, Richmond, 1995.

9 As for example when the Vatican and a group of Muslim governments worked together to oppose certain policies at the conference on population control in Cairo in 1994.

Select Bibliography

Khurshid Ahman, 'Islam and the West: Confrontation or Co-operation?', *The Muslim World*, vol. LXXXV, No. 1–2, January–April, 1995, pp. 63–81.

Munawar Ahmad Anees, Syed Z. Abedin and Ziauddin Sardar, *Christian–Muslim Relations: Yesterday, Today and Tomorrow*, Grey Seal, London, 1991.

M.A. Bari, 'Muslim Demands for their own Denominational Schools in the United Kingdom', *Muslim Educational Quarterly*, vol. 10, No. 2, 1993, pp. 62–72.

Norman Daniels, *Islam and the West: The Making of an Image*, Edinburgh University Press, Edinburgh, 1960, 1962, 1966 and 1980.

Kevin Dwyer, *Arab Voices: The Human Rights Debate in the Middle East*, Routledge, London, 1991.

John L. Esposito, *The Islamic Threat: Myth or Reality?*, Oxford University Press, Oxford, 1992.

Jean-Marie Gaudeul, *Encounters and Clashes: Islam and Christianity in History*, Pontifical Institute for Arabic and Islamic Studies, Rome, 1984, vol. 1.

Hugh Goddard, *Christians and Muslims: From Double Standards to Mutual Understanding*, Curzon Press, Richmond, 1995.

Fred Halliday, *Islam and the Myth of Confrontation: Religion and Politics in the Middle East*, I.B. Tauris, London, 1995.

Ali Köse, *Conversion to Islam: A Study of Native British Converts*, Kegan Paul, London and New York, 1996.

Nehemiah Levtzion, ed., *Towards a Comparative Study of Islamization*, Holmes and Meier Publishers, 1979.

Philip Lewis, *Islamic Britain: Religion, Politics and Identity among British Muslims*, I.B. Tauris, London, 1994.

Elizabeth Ann Meyer, *Islam and Human Rights: Tradition and Politics*, Westview Press, Boulder and San Francisco, Pinter Publishers, London, 1995.

Seyyed Hossein Nasr, 'Islam and the West: Yesterday and Today', *Q-News International*, No. 248–250, 27 Dec 1996–9 Jan 1997, pp. 10–13, and 41.

Larry Poston, *Islamic Da'wah in the West: Muslim Missionary Activity and the Dynamics of Conversion to Islam*, Oxford University Press, Oxford, 1992.

Olivier Roy, *The Failure of Political Islam*, I.B. Tauris, London, 1994.

Lamin Sanneh, 'Can A House Divided Stand? Reflections on Christian–Muslim Encounter in the West', *International Bulletin of Missionary Research*, October, 1993, pp. 164–168.

Johannes Schwartlander and Heiner Bielefeldt, *Christians and Muslims Facing the Challenge of Human Rights*, German Bishops' Conference Research Group on the Universal Tasks of the Church, Bonn, 1994.

Ataullah Siddiqui, *Christian–Muslim Dialogue in the Twentieth Century*, Macmillan, London, 1997.

Rotraud Wielandt, 'Islamic Religious Education in a Pluralist Society', *British Journal of Religious Education*, vol. 15, No. 2, Spring, 1993, pp. 50–57.

Kate Zebiri, *Muslims and Christians Face to Face*, One World, Oxford, 1997.